Published by MENTALIZER™, CORP.
Mentalizer Education.
450 West 58th Street, Suite 1H
New York, NY 10019
Visit our Web site at www.mentalizer.com

Originally published in hardcover by CreateSpace, November 2013.
First Edition: November 2013.
Photographs by Shutterstock.

ISBN-13: 978-1494208271

ISBN-10: 149420827X

SECRETS
OF THE VOICE

or

READ PEOPLE BASED
ON THEIR VOICES
and
INFLUENCE OTHERS
USING YOUR OWN VOICE

By
Ehud Segev
The Mentalizer

Published by Mentalizer Education

Table of Contents

Ehud Segev, The Mentalizer

About the author

World-renowned mentalist Ehud Segev, aka The Mentalizer, was born in 1979 in the Israeli city of Safed, long known as the spiritual center of the Jewish world. In the 16th century, Safed emerged as the city of Kabbalah, the oldest and most influential wisdom of mysticism. Most of the great scholars and Rabbis who studied and taught the secrets of Kabbalah lived in this great city, and it is also where Ehud Segev began his spiritual destiny. Ehud the "Mentalizer" (mental analyzer) combines his acting skills with his special, strong connection to people in order to provide entertainment, as well as deeper understanding of human psychology and behavior.

Growing up in the Upper Galilee in the 1980s, Ehud chose to spend his time unlike other boys his age. While neighborhood kids were outside playing, 12-year-old Segev was inside reading books on mind reading, non-verbal behavior, and the Kabbalah. Though the town's librarian was alarmed to see such a young boy delve into esoteric mysticism, Ehud's mother was not; she has always known there was something different about her son.

"When I was twelve, I took the entire shelf of books that dealt with mysticism and spiritualism from the library, and my mother had to sign a permission form since I was too young for this topic," Ehud recalls. "The librarian thought I lost my mind, but my mother was ever so supportive. I'll never forget that."

His reputation for having a connection to the universe, combined with his ability to read minds, analyze behavior, and influence people, had set the stage for his worldwide success. At 16, Ehud was featured on the news for his special ability, one that some people consider magic, while others believe it is spiritual. Segev has another way of explaining it, referring to his gift as "magic from the mind."

"Others call it intuition. I don't. I call it the 'knowledge to connect'," he explains. "The more YOU KNOW, the more you're able to connect to yourself and to others. And the more you are connected, the bigger the miracles that you can perform. I don't have any **super**natural powers; on the contrary— my powers are **natural** it's super!

In my shows and lectures throughout the world, I combine my special abilities as a performer with magic and spirituality. My goal: to make this world a better place and to help people realize that our deepest desires aren't materialistic, but spiritual. If I can use all the publicity, the stage-presence and my TV appearances to bring people closer to the light, my destiny is fulfilled."

Fascination with Segev continued when, at 19, he accurately predicted who would win the race for the mayors' chair in several cities. This prediction was made in a newspaper article titled "The Prophecy", which was published 11 days before the elections. With only a photo as reference, Ehud used his mentalism abilities to analyze each candidate and foresee the winners. "When I turned out to be right, people started calling me the Mental Analyzer, and soon nicknamed me The Mentalizer," he says.

A couple of years later, Ehud became one of the small number of entertainers who signed an exclusive contract with the US Army to entertain troops in bases around the world. For this he received a coin of excellence - a special award for extraordinary contribution - which was the basis for accepting the EB-1 classification from the US Department of Homeland Security and becoming a permanent resident in America. To qualify for the prestigious EB-1 classification, a person must have an extraordinary ability and be "one of that small percentage who have risen to the very top of the field of endeavor" according to the USCIS documentation.

Now performing in shows around the world, including being featured on shows such as NBC's series "Phenomenon," as well as on numerous Israeli television networks, Ehud's reputation remains positive. He is concerned with providing his audiences with more than just entertainment - his goal is to give people who watch his shows a deeper understanding of human nature, and help them develop self-awareness and consciousness.

He also seeks to help people understand how they can use some of his techniques in their own lives through his program **"How to Be a Mental Analyzer."** The program is based on in-depth studies of human behavior patterns and the psyche, and covers techniques such as neuro-linguistic programming, body language interpretation, voice analysis, meditation, and self-hypnosis – among others - to enhance daily interactions in the workplace and home, and become happier and more successful in general.

His belief is that these abilities can be used by anyone to spread positive energies in the world and better serve humanity, one person at a time.

"In our own way, each one of us is a prophet and each one of us is a leader and a follower - it's just about using all the techniques outlined in the program. Everyone can learn how to take advantage of these tools," Ehud says.

This is his second published book. The first one, **"9 Steps to Influence,"** became an *Amazon bestseller* in less than 48 hours!

THANK YOU FOR PURCHASING THIS BOOK!

PLEASE SURF TO:

www.5j.biz/voice/gift

**AND GET A SPECIAL THANK YOU GIFT
JUST BECAUSE YOU'RE IMPORTANT TO US!**

Introduction:
Your voice is speaking volumes

"Words mean more than what is set down on paper. It takes the human voice to infuse them with deeper meaning."

-- *American poet, Maya Angelou*

Even before we are born, we are listening for voices. Researchers found that an unborn baby shows a marked preference for a mother's voice - one of the few sensory perceptions accessible in the womb. Once born, the infant remains sensitive to the sound of voices she hears around her, and even though she hasn't yet developed the ability to interpret vocal variations, she instinctively reacts (happily) to a soothing voice, and (not so happily) to a loud or harsh one.

That beginning of a life cycle is also the start of our communication with others. It will develop as we grow older, becoming more discernible and defined.

But have you ever wondered what our world would be like if human beings couldn't communicate with each other? You wouldn't be able to tell someone you love him or her. You wouldn't be able to share your innermost thoughts and emotions with people closest to you. You wouldn't be able to have any impact or influence on anyone, as though you didn't really exist and your opinions and feelings didn't matter.

Unthinkable, isn't it? That's because effective communication is the cornerstone on which good relationships are built. And, good relationships – whether personal or professional – are the foundation of a happy and successful life.

This is a good place to mention **Helen Keller**. She was born blind and deaf in the second half of the 19th century, but had overcome these disabilities to becoming a writer and lecturer.

When asked which of her two impairments affected her more, she answered: *"Blindness separates people from things, but deafness separates people from people."*

Think about it: most people, if asked which is a worse disability – blindness or deafness – would probably choose the former. But Helen, who was afflicted by both, considered her inability to hear voices of people around her to be a more severe handicap. **Because, if you can't hear a person's voice, how can you know what he or she is thinking and feeling?**

Let me give you another example. A friend was telling me how she "met" her husband. The two were introduced on the Internet by mutual friends but couldn't meet in person for several weeks because they lived hundreds of kilometers apart from each other. So they conducted their "courtship" on the phone.

I asked her why they didn't Skype so they could at least see each other, and she answered that she wanted to get to know him through the sound of his voice.

Why? Because, she said, the voice gave her good indication of what kind of person the young man was. She was able to judge his personality by how he sounded! (Once you start reading this book, you'll find out what cues she was looking for to assess his personality).

This book is titled **"Secrets of the Voice"** and it is written by **Ehud Segev the Mentalizer** ("Mentalizer," by the way, is combination of two words – "mental" and "analyzer" – someone who uses a variety of skills and abilities to understand, interpret, and influence human behavior.)

You might be wondering what is so "secret" about the voice? After all, we all use it every day. We communicate with it and with non-verbal means like a touch, eye contact, gestures, and other body language signals.

All that is true, but your voice is so much more than just "another means of communication." Yes, your voice has secrets! Success or failure is often determined not simply by what we say, but how we say it. Therefore, the voice is our single most important communication tool. It defines who we are and affects how others respond to us, and how powerfully it shapes our everyday world.

Before we explore, in this book, the intriguing facts about the human voice, consider this:

About 93 percent of human communication is derived from a non-verbal language - 55 percent of it is facial expressions, gestures, as well as body posture and position; 38 percent is the vocal communication and only 7 percent is pure verbal communication, meaning - the spoken word. This became known as the 55-38-7 rule, put forth by Professor **Albert Mehrabian** of **UCLA**, who came up with the scientific proofs for this phenomena.

Given these numbers, you might be wondering whether you can make a lasting (and, hopefully, positive) impression on other people through a spoken word.

Can it make a significant impact on the way we understand other people and are understood ourselves? The answer is **yes** and **yes** - as long as you grasp the importance of voice and learn how to make yours a potent one!

Basically your words only affect 7 percent of your audience's reaction to you, but combined with the other 38 percent of vocal communication, you'll be able to use your spoken word and voice to control and influence others in a positive way.

We heard about people who could hypnotize others in a matter of seconds just by saying a few words in their ears.

Well, not sure if this is true or just a tale, but the bottom line is that by the time you finish reading my book, you'll be many steps ahead in the game and you'll be able to analyze others as well as influence them using the voice and the voice only.

You might be thinking: **"a voice is a voice, so what's the big deal?"** Well, it IS a big deal. Did you know that speech, and human voice in general, is an amazing tool even though we tend to take it for granted?

It has evolved over the millennia of evolution, from primitive grunts of our early ancestors to the sounds we hear today.

And it is not haphazard: every sound you make requires a precise coordination of your head, neck, chest, and abdominal muscles. I bet you never thought of your voice that way, have you?

As you will learn from this book, your voice is a very important communication tool. It makes it possible for us to interact with each other, especially in situations in which we can't rely on body language – yes, even when speaking on the phone, talking to a young child who has not yet learned to interpret body language signals, or a sight- impaired person who relies on the sound of your voice to understand you.

Last but certainly not least, the voice can have a powerful emotional impact - it can touch, move, influence, or inspire us. To illustrate this point, let me tell you a story related to me by a friend who had lost her father. She thought about him a lot and, even as time went by, missed him very much. One day, after she got home from work, she noticed that the light on her landline answering machine was blinking, signaling a message.

Since my friend uses her mobile phone and only rarely the landline, she saw that the message was from the previous year.

When she clicked the button to play it, she heard the voice of her deceased father, recorded just weeks before his death. He was conveying some news about a relative.

My friend was, of course, shocked to hear her dad's voice, but also comforted. Sure, she had plenty of photographs of her father, but actually hearing his voice was so much more - as she describes it - **"vivid and intense."**

Generally speaking, the sound of the voice can bring on a wide range of emotional reactions, both positive and negative. They can run a gamut from happiness and contentment to hostility and anger.

It all depends on five components, which I will briefly outline in a few minutes and which will be elaborated and explained in detail throughout this book.

For a mentalist like myself, a spoken word is an important tool as well, not only to project a certain stage presence – the ability to command the attention and impress people around me – but also to influence them through the different elements of my voice.

In this book, you will get a comprehensive overview of the impact your voice can have on others, and vice-versa. You'll be surprised!

The voice tells all!

What do you do when someone speaks to you? The obvious answer is - you **LISTEN**. And that, dear friend, is one of the most essential skills a mentalizer - and all human beings, for that matter - should develop.

Because if you know how to LISTEN intently and attentively, you will not only begin to understand other people's thoughts and feelings (and thus get to know their inner selves), but also be able to distill important clues, cues, and signals people are giving you, most often without even realizing it.

In that way, a voice is not merely a tool to convey messages; it is also a way of knowing what is on people's minds. And, once you learn how to master your own voice, you can start to influence everyone around you - in a positive way, of course! That's what I mean when I say **"the voice tells all."**

You probably already know how to interpret the most common intonations: a soft whisper is gentle on the ears and conveys a degree of intimacy and inner peace. A raised voice, on the other hand, imparts irritation, anger, and aggressiveness. Needless to say, we all prefer a calm, even-toned, and melodious voice than **YELLING!** You don't have to be a body language specialist to know that an extremely loud voice (unless you happen to be an opera singer) is, in most situations, unpleasant and nerve-wracking.

You can actually ensure that your message compels and excites your listeners by making your voice more expressive. What does this mean? An expressive voice is not "static." Rather, it changes – ebbs, flows, and recedes - depending on the feelings you are trying to convey – it pauses and quickens ... changes pace ... lowers and raises both volume and pitch. This sounds almost poetic, doesn't it?

I am giving you these obvious examples because I want you to thoroughly understand the importance of your voice. Your voice can definitely have either a positive or negative effect on how people perceive you and relate to you. And as a mentalizer, you'll have to master this aspect because it'll give you power over other people - whether you're using your own voice to control the people around you, or using your expertise to unlock the psychology behind the way they talk.

This is a crucial element in becoming a mentalizer so I decided to put all the effort I can into this book and split it into five main topics where I will concentrate on how to master and understand each vocal component.

I divided each topic into short and to the point chapters to keep this book a handy guide that is *SUPER EASY* to follow and master!

A distinct voice of your own

As stated above, a human voice conveys many different emotions. In the best of cases, it will express your passion and enthusiasm, but it can also reflect pain and sadness. That is why the mentalizer's ability to listen is crucial – your ear and brain will capture not just what the words convey, but also what the voice "tells" you (which may be something completely different).

For instance, a person who wants to hide her true feelings might say, **"I am happy,"** but the elements of her voice will send out a message that she is sad. Just as interpreting the gestures, posture, and facial expressions can help you assess someone's state of mind, so can the intonation, inflection, modulation, and pacing of the voice.

In other words (no pun intended!), a mentalizer can't just learn to understand the ins and outs of the body language without also mastering the nuances of the voice. If you do one without the other, your **"mentalizer tool kit"** will have a gaping hole in it!

Now, once you'll master the five elements I will teach you in this book, your world will open up.

Not only will you be able to read between the lines, but you'll also be able to analyze and understand the true meanings of certain conversations.

You'll soon discover that sometimes people's words and sentences don't reveal what they are **really** trying to convey, but have a hidden meaning. As an example, when the plumber tells you, **"The pipe was broken and I had to work so hard to fix it, so you need to pay 100 dollars,"** you'll be able to know he is actually saying *"Everything was fine, I solved it easily and you should be paying 50 bucks but I'm going to try and get 100!"*

Most people who are not mentalizers probably don't realize that their voice has many components to it. They may know there are different singing voices – like soprano, tenor, baritone, etc. – but not that our speaking voices have an exciting life of their own too.

Paypee Tovary the great wizard

Now I will teach you a secret spell, a wizard's name… practice it until you say it perfectly: **"Paypee Tovary"** or *Paypee Tow Vahree*. It is pronounced like **"Pay** *(like pay)* **Tow** *(like tow)* **Va** *(like the beginning of the word Valentine)* and **Ree** *(as in Read)*.

Now that you've learned this phrase I want you to practice saying it a few times. In the beginning it'll sound weird and you won't understand why the hell I taught you how to say it.

Are you confused by this exercise?

Don't be!

Paypee Tovary is a mnemonic system I came up with to memorize the five elements you'll have to master. For a beginner mentalizer, it'll be hard to dissect the different elements when you talk/listen, so you'll have to recall each and every one of them. Want to know the elements I'm talking about?

They are:

• **Pace**

• **Pitch**

• **Tone**

• **Volume**

• **Rhythm**

These five major components are clear indicators of our emotional state, mood, and thoughts and you are about to master them so you'll get so much closer to being a great mentalizer.

And here comes the mnemonic technique I taught you: **Paypee Tovary** is the first syllable of each one of the components added together.

So once you memorize the face of the great wizard, you'll be able to know how to call him every time you'll need to analyze someone's speech, or prepare your own.

Let's see it in action:

Pace is the speed (or the slowness) with which you speak.

Pitch is how high or low your voice sounds in a given situation – an indication of your emotional state at that particular time.

Tone is an "attitude" (both good and bad) that is expressed in your voice. Think about the expression **"I didn't like his tone of voice."** So yes – it's not only *WHAT* you say, but also *HOW* you say it.

Volume is how quietly or loud you speak – whispers, yells, and all the vocal ranges in between.

Rhythm is the evenness or unevenness of your voice.

All of the above components are important parts of oral communication - **"the body language of the voice."**

I know it might sound a bit overwhelming, especially the idea to comprehend all these different elements **EVERY TIME** someone is speaking to you! But this is why, throughout the next chapters, we will study together each aspect of this subject, which I will present to you in the simplest terms possible. I strongly suggest that you give yourself time to exercise and master each component before you move on to the next one.

It will be easier and less overwhelming for you to proceed this way.

Videos

Since this book is about the voice, it was important to me to make it an interactive experience for my readers. This is why I added many online videos to support what we learn here.

So basically, the process of reading this book should be side-by-side with the Internet access which most of you have. In fact, I made it truly simple for you to follow the videos embedded in this book! Every time a video will be featured you'll have a hyperlink next to it with the video's ID number.

You're invited to surf to our book's video page at the simple website address: **www.5j.biz/voice/**

In this page you'll have a list of ALL the video links by their numeric order and you can either follow along with your computer, or by clicking the link on your tablet (as long as it supports it). I hope you'll enjoy this great feature!

Words...

Have you ever heard of a French singer named **F. R. David**? If you haven't, don't worry – I think most people outside of **France** don't know anything about him.

Why am I mentioning him? In 1988, his song, "Words" sold 8 million records and topped various charts around Europe. It is a sweet and melodic tune, and you can hear it here:

 1 | www.5j.biz/voice/1

The reason I am talking about this song is because of its opening and refrain lyrics:

"Words don't come easy to me

How can I find a way to make you see I love you."

Clearly, F. D. David wasn't aware of the fact that **"words"** are not the only way to express love or, for that matter, other emotions. As you will learn from this book, **VOICE**, and all its five components, which will be discussed here in detail, is an essential part of communicating feelings and ideas. Words alone can never adequately or accurately convey our innermost thoughts.

This is **NOT** to say that someone who is articulate and well spoken can't express himself with clarity. All that this means is that in order to communicate with as much impact as possible, we must pay attention not just to **WHAT** we say but also **HOW** we say it –through the pitch, tone, volume, pace, and rhythm.

To make this learning process as complete as possible, each chapter will cover two aspects of every vocal component: the inside aspect (how to use you own voice to its fullest potential), and the outside one about analyzing other people's voices in order to understand their thoughts and emotions.

In order to make this experience even more effective, I recommend that you purchase a software called **"The Passaggio Vocal Feedback System"** (it's the best $19 dollars you'll ever spend! And you can download it from **5j.biz/voice/system**) Why? Because it will be an essential tool to help you visually work your way in understanding the different aspects of the voice.

As you learn how to feel and observe things like pitch and volume, this software will help you to grasp these concepts faster. I will show you in the next lessons how to use this software to achieve greatness in your own speeches or when recording others - even people you hear on TV!

It was originally designed for singers, but I'm taking advantage of the visual tool it provides to teach aspiring mentalizers how to understand the voice mechanics.

Yes, nobody knows it but I basically use *"an innocent singers"* software to serve as my personal voice assistant (don't tell the wizard Paypee Tovary - he'll be mad at me). The truth is that even the best mentalizers can use some **VISUAL** help when it comes to mentalizing the features of the human voice. And this software just nails these features and it's like a **"secret tool"** that you can use too!

When we are done exploring each vocal component mentioned above, you will be in for a treat: a BONUS chapter teaching you how to use everything you have learned in this book to give a compelling presentation – either at work or in social interactions. I don't have to tell you how important this information is and how useful it can be in creating good impressions, building strong (professional and personal) relationships, and positively influencing people around you. Yes, the **SECRETS OF THE VOICE** will unlock the power of **EFFECTIVE COMMUNICATION!**

So are you ready to start? Great! You'll have fun learning secrets of the human voice - **YOUR** voice – and discovering what messages, emotions and thoughts, are discernible through speech. I will also share specific techniques on interpreting someone's voice, as well as controlling your own. You'll feel how your power will grow and expand after each lesson you master! But before we begin, I'd like to tell you a personal story that, I hope, will inspire you and help you along the path of learning about this fascinating subject.

Listen to this!

Back when I was just a little boy in Israel, my kindergarten teacher sat my parents down one day and broke this news to them:

"Your son, Ehud, is deaf!"

Needless to say, mom and dad were stunned and asked for an explanation. **"He doesn't hear a word I am saying nor can he hear the other teachers or his friends talking,"** she offered. **"He is not speaking or participating at all. He lives in his own world – not connected. He might have a mental disability of some sort. I'm not sure if this boy can stay in this kindergarten – he might need a special program."**

I heard every word she said with perfect clarity!

Actually, the teacher wasn't completely wrong. I may have appeared as someone who was hard of hearing because I didn't respond or react to anything she was saying. I did act as though I were disconnected from and oblivious to reality. Truth is, I was living in a mysterious world of my own and harboring a secret...

What secret, you may ask? I will tell you: even as a child, I was so focused on observing, registering, and analyzing everything around me that I didn't pay any attention to my teacher – or other people, for that matter.

To the teacher, I seemed to be the exact opposite of an ordinary child – in all likelihood, she never came across a strange kid like myself! And looking back at it now, my behavior probably was weird (at least to an outside observer). But to me, this intense focus on things and people that surrounded me was totally normal.

You see, I felt a need to develop my inner awareness so that I could better understand and interpret the world around me. In fact, I was listening – and watching - attentively in order to learn what was really going on in everyone's mind (except my teacher's!)

This precocious curiosity was the cornerstone on which my abilities as a mentalizer were built. With time, I put little pieces of the puzzle together, sharpening my mind's acuity, and developing my observation and analysis skills. I was just like the owl in this ancient Chinese saying:

"A wise old owl sat on an oak;

The more he saw the less he spoke;

The less he spoke the more he heard;

Why aren't we like that wise old bird?"

Now that you know my **"secret"** (that I wasn't really deaf – just concentrating on the sounds, sights, and sensations surrounding me), you might be wondering why I am telling you this story in a book that is about the voice.

Read on, and you will find out...

Open up your ears!

In one episode of the TV show **"The Mentalist,"** **Patrick Jane** (played by **Simon Baker**), is asked by someone who is amazed by his abilities: *"Are you a psychic?"* Patrick replies: *"No, but I know how to listen!"*

And that, dear friend, is one of the most important **"tools"** a mentalizer – and **ALL** people - should possess. Unfortunately, this is often not the case.

Why am I bringing up the importance of listening when the topic of this book is voice interpretation?

Well, it goes without saying that before you can even start to analyze someone's voice, **you have to hear it clearly** first. This is where the ability to <u>LISTEN</u> is really, really important – in fact, you can't aspire to be a mentalizer if you don't listen! (Now you understand my personal story, as related above).

Now, you might say, *"Of course I listen."* But, do you **really**?

Ask yourself this question: **how much of what you hear you actually remember?** Chances are you only retain a small part of what people tell you. In fact, studies suggest that we remember only between 25 percent and 50 percent of what we hear. In other words, we forget between half and three-quarters of the things people tell us – as the saying goes, **"in one ear and out the other."**

So listening is not just nodding your head and pretending to hear what someone tells you, while your mind jumps all over the place. **That's NOT enough!**

Listening, really listening is paying attention, showing genuine interest, openness and curiosity in what other people tell you. And, for the purpose of this book, listening carefully is the only way you can interpret the nuances of someone's voice. I learned this as a child by listening to everything and everyone around me – even though my teacher believed I was deaf!

Valuable knowledge

As you continue to read this book and learn more about the **pitch, tone, volume, rhythm, and pace,** you will understand how essential good listening skills are. Just as you depend on a keen eye to observe various visual signals, you also need a pair of alert ears to hear the cues emitted by the above-mentioned vocal components.

A friend of mine, who is a psychotherapist, told me that the most challenging part of his job – aside from treating people who are going through various difficulties - is the art of listening. **"Before I started this work, I had no idea how much effort and energy it takes to listen to what patients tell me,"** he says.

But what if you are not a natural-born listener? Don't worry, you can develop this skill through several simple techniques. They are easy to learn, but you would be surprised - maybe even shocked - at how many people don't even try to master them. Yes, it does take some work (as my psychotherapist friend had discovered), but everything in life that is important and worthwhile requires some effort, mostly in the form of practice and exercise.

So how can you go about sharpening your listening skills and use them to "read" vocal clues just like Patrick Jane "The Mentalist" does? Yes, it is possible, though, in all likelihood, you will **not** have a television show of your own.

Become more aware

There are several progressive and gradual techniques to boost your listening ability. By "**progressive and gradual,**" I mean you should proceed step-by-step, because each one will make it easier to learn the next.

In a few moments I will show you how to develop your listening skills. But before doing so, there are other, very important skills you must master: **FOCUS, OBSERVE,** and **PAY ATTENTION!**

Let's explore it.

Focus. This ability is, in a way, a springboard for all the other skills necessary for the voice analysis. That's because if you can't focus effectively, you won't be able to observe or pay attention, and, in turn, analyze voices.

Here's something you probably already know: getting your mind to focus on one thing – action, thought, or sensation – at a time, is not easy. We are so accustomed to multi-tasking that our brain is – in a manner of speaking – all over the place. You might think that you accomplish much more by doing several tasks at the same time, and maybe that's true. But your poor brain becomes so used to distractions coming at it from all sides, that it is not able to concentrate on just one thing.

The human brain is not programmed to deal with this onslaught. Think of your mind as a garden, which is overgrown with weeds that take up every inch of space. Before you can plant anything new in it, you must first remove all those wild plants that leave no room for anything else. So, in order to boost your focusing ability, you must clear your brain of all the trash that's polluting it. That junk that sits in there - too much TV, computer games, emails, voicemails, and all the other information assaulting us from left and right - clutters your brain and dulls all the senses a mentalizer should possess: sharp powers of observation, great memory, acuity, as well as physical and emotional awareness. **How can you learn to de-clutter your brain?** First, you have to give up old habits and adapt some new ones. You can start by:

• **Prioritizing** your tasks and consciously paying your full attention to just one thing at a time. In the beginning it may be difficult not to get distracted but if you keep at it, you'll get better. (You might call it "having a one-track mind").

• Having a **"tunnel vision,"** which means looking at just one thing at a time rather than letting your eyes dart all over the place. Train your mind to remember all the details about just ONE object: its color, shape, and fragrance – whatever.

• **Meditating.** It may not be easy at first, but if you learn to do this even for brief moments each day, you'll derive numerous benefits, from better concentration to inner peace.

Once you learn to clear your mind and are able to focus effectively, you are ready to start listening!

Be ACTIVE!

One effective technique that teaches you to "catch" all the essential elements of voice analysis (after your brain has been cleared) is the so-called **"active listening."** It could also be called **"conscious"** listening, because you must really concentrate on and pay full attention to what you are hearing. This technique may not come naturally or even easily to many people because, as mentioned previously, we've accustomed our brains to multitask. But here's what you can try to do, little by little but on regular basis, to become an active listener:

• After using mind-decluttering techniques explained above, sit down with another person and listen carefully, attentively, and consciously to the pattern of his or her voice. (In the following chapters you will learn to interpret the pitch, tone, volume, rhythm, and pace, but for now, you are developing your listening skills).

• Don't interrupt or jump in mid-sentence – you are **not** listening in order to reply, but in order to **learn to interpret vocal patterns.**

The ability to **FOCUS, LISTEN, OBSERVE,** and **UNDERSTAND** is the key that opens up the fascinating world of voice analysis – and Mentalism in general. Please practice all the techniques mentioned above before you start reading the next chapter, which is all about...**pitching!**

PITCH

The Pitch

Have you ever noticed how people are concerned about how they look, but don't pay as much attention to what they sound like? **BIG** mistake, if you ask me!

To our subconscious minds, the quality of a voice is very important; in fact, it can make as much of (positive or negative) impression on other people as one's physical appearance.

And that is why – as explained previously – the vocal pitch, pace, volume, rhythm, and tone really do matter and determine how people react and respond to your ideas.

In this chapter we will focus on the pitch (with further ones covering the four other vocal components).

Why is the pitch of your voice important, you may wonder, and why do other people judge your behavior and personality by how you sound?

That is a very good question and some answers will be given to you right here in this chapter.

Also, since **SHOWING** is so much more effective than merely **TELLING**, I am providing here some specific video examples and experiments in pitch, so that the whole concept is easier to understand.

And, you will also find some proven techniques on controlling your own pitch, so you are able to make a great impression on people – especially if you also master all the other voice components I'll focus on in the next chapters.

Before we begin, let me add that throughout these lessons, we will focus only on **SPEAKING** voices – not the singing ones or the voices you might be hearing in your head (neither of these falls under my area of expertise) Okay, let's start... pitching!

Good vibrations

Before we get into the nitty-gritty of human pitches, let's have a quick overview. First, you might be wondering why men have (usually) lower pitches than women. That's because the rate of vibration depends largely on the length and thickness of the vocal cords, and women generally have shorter vocal cords than men.

Of course, there are variations within each gender as well, which is why all women's voices and all men's voices don't sound exactly the same.

Another thing to remember is that in a course of a day the pitch changes – a phenomenon called "inflection." The voice fluctuates depending on what we are thinking and feeling; most people don't speak in a monotonous, robotic pitch all the time.

Adult voices have different pitches – from very high to very low, and ranges in between. Let's understand for a second how the pitch is being determined: through **VIBRATIONS**.

Vibrations of the vocal cords determine the pitch – the greater the rate of vibrations per second, the higher the pitch.

The opposite is true as well: if the number of vibrations is lower, so is the pitch, resulting in a deep, booming voice.

As **Nikola Tesla**, a great 19th century electrical inventor put it:

"If you want to find the secrets of the universe, think in terms of energy, frequency and VIBRATION."

Here's a great example of how vibrations influence the world:

 2 | www.5j.biz/voice/2

What you see above is a beautiful old video from 1933 that shows sound waves and their sources (this movie is part of the collection: *Prelinger Archives*).

The **tuning fork** is one of the greatest ways to explain the vibrations passing through space when a certain tone is being created. We will talk more about this in the **TONE** lesson, but for now we want to concentrate on the pitch of the voice.

I want you to see how the pitch influences the listener. We want to see it visually before we hear it, so here's a beautiful experiment that shows you how the vibrations of a certain frequency affect the surrounding.

The experiment you will see in this next video is called the **"Chladni Plate Experiment."** A tone generator was used with a wave driver (speaker) and a metal plate attached to the speaker.

First they added sand to the plate then began playing a tone. Certain frequencies vibrate the metal plate in such a way that it creates areas where there is no vibration. The sand "falls" into those areas, creating beautiful geometric patterns. As the frequency increases in pitch the patterns become more complex.

 **3 | www.5j.biz/voice/3**

Notice what happens in the space above the speaker. The vibrations are there. They create the amazing shapes you can see, so you understand that the vibrations our pitch is creating influence the space that surrounds us.

Can you imagine how your pitch affects the people around you? Even when we don't consciously understand why we feel a certain way when we hear someone speak, our sub-consciousness is absorbing the voice and shapes our feelings towards that certain person!

Now that you know how the pitches are produced in the vocal cords, let's look at what messages they convey.

Keep it low!

Y ou might not have paid attention to vocal pitches in the past, but now you will hopefully realize that the pitch of the voice (along with the other four components as shown by the wizard Paypee Tovary) sends out messages about the person's mood and state of mind just as clearly as non-verbal gestures and facial expressions do. That's because in any given situation, the pitch of your voice is determined by your emotions.

Please understand that for most people, this is an instinctual reflex, something they don't consciously think about or control. But those of us who are skilled in interpreting body language – both spoken and non-verbal – can deduce someone's state of mind just by listening to the voice. **Let's look at a few examples:**

• A person who is calm and in control of him/herself, will have a steady pitch, within the lower vocal range.

• An anxious or insecure person, on the other hand, will probably produce a high, quivering pitch. An expert in communications and/or voice analysis will immediately know what you are feeling at that particular moment.

• Generally speaking, people prefer to listen to a lower-pitched voice, because the person comes across as stable and reliable; the high range signals someone who is excitable, tense, and emotionally **"all over the place."**

Did he kill her?

I wanted to show you this in action so I searched the web for a **"murder interview"** in order to explore the pitch of the person talking and analyze is with my readers. Here is the clip that came up:

4 | www.5j.biz/voice/4

In August 2012, with schoolgirl **Tia Sharp** still missing, **Stuart Hazell** told **ITV News** that he had no involvement in her disappearance.

Hazell, 37, had denied killing the girl and hiding her body in the attic of the house he shared with his former partner, **Christine Bicknell** — Tia's grandmother. But on the fifth day of his trial, he dramatically changed his plea and admitted to murdering her.

This television interview, in which Hazell angrily refuted allegations that he had anything to do with Tia's disappearance, was broadcast in August 2012 as police and volunteers searched for the missing child.

This will be a wonderful exercise for you, and also a great way of realizing how strongly emotions affect the pitch. As you concentrate on the pitch of

Hazell's voice, you'll discover that every time he lies and gets uncomfortable his pitch goes up - especially when he is describing the situation as **"horrible"** and saying that the family was stuck inside with the papers outside accusing him.

Keep listening and watching till the end. Dissect the elements and concentrate only on the pitch. You'll notice that most of the time (for almost three minutes) he recalls **"real"** memories and his pitch is mostly steady, but at 2:50 he starts losing it by facing reality and his pitch goes **higher and higher.**

Remember: as you continue learning, you'll have the ability to notice changes in people, and determine whether they are lying or telling the truth, based on their pitch alone.

Ask yourself: how do **YOU** want to be seen (or heard) by others? If you opt for the lower pitch (and of course you should because you want to come across as someone who is credible and in control of his emotions), how can you learn to manage your voice effectively?

There are some techniques used by professional performers, public speakers, and other people who want to be perceived as competent, trustworthy, persuasive and influential – we'll cover them in the bonus chapter at the end of this book.

Good news is that even though you are not a voice expert now, you can learn and become a pro.

It's all a matter of practice!

Changing your pitch...

I'd like to share this story with you: One of the speakers I met wasn't too successful. When she started her speech, people used to walk out annoyed. She was really upset and when we met she asked for my advice.

The reason why people left the room was because they felt as though they were being treated like fools. Her pitch was very high and her intonation was that of a kindergarten teacher speaking to little children - condescending and irritating at the same time. So although the content she provided had great value for her listeners, they just couldn't stand the pitch and intonation, so the message she wanted to convey didn't get through to her audience.

She was very happy that I was honest (and maybe even a bit cruel) and had told her the truth rather than sugarcoating the message. She started practicing a new way of speaking. Her pitch went down an octave, and her rhythm and intonation became much more friendly, although still authoritative.

The change was huge. People would stay throughout her entire lecture and come to her afterwards, hugging her, and telling her how she completely changed their lives with her knowledge.

Remember: the content she was providing was the same, but her delivery changed.

So you see, your pitch will determine whether someone will listen to you or not.

Let's bring in a bit of humor here to make my point even clearer. Would you want to listen to this pitch for more than a few seconds?

 **5 | www.5j.biz/voice/5**

No? I can't blame you!

Monotone pitch

A monotone – pitch that is flat, unchanging and without intonation - will most likely make people ignore you because they will be bored – in fact, they may fall asleep listening to you.

Just look at this scene from a very funny movie, **"Ferris Bueller's Day Off:"**

 6 | www.5j.biz/voice/6

I don't know what is more irritating – **Donald Duck** or this teacher's flat and lifeless voice!

Why is the monotone so ineffective?

<u>Well, it's quite simple:</u> when people hear a voice like the one in the video, with no highlights or emphasis on certain words, they tune out. The only message they receive is this: since the speech is lifeless, their subconscious is telling them that the content is dull as well. And if that's the case, your audience is *"falling asleep"* as you talk. They predict that your speech will not provide anything interesting so they don't listen. All this stresses the importance of learning how to use your pitch in order to engage your listeners and keep them enthralled as you speak!

It's all about the pitch, baby!

When you are stressed, nervous or anxious, your throat tenses and vocal cords constrict, lowering the pitch. Here are a few steps you can take to loosen your throat muscles and vocal cords, so you don't sound like Donald Duck.

• Before meeting with people where good impressions count, drink something warm. Avoid cold fluids because they tighten your vocal cords; warm water or tea will soothe the cords and throat, and generally relax you. Don't drink MILK or dairy drinks (such as Yogurt, coffee with milk etc.) because milk creates mucus, which interferes with your vocal performance. You can drink all the milk you want, anytime, but not before an important speech / interview / etc.

• Relaxation techniques such as deep breathing will also loosen tight muscles – not just in your throat, but also in your chest, shoulders, abdomen, and other parts of the body that impact your voice. Here's how it works:

Sit comfortably and let all your muscles relax. Imagine the tension evaporating from your neck, shoulders, abdominal area, legs, and any other part of your body that is tight.

Close your eyes and imagine a soothing color. This visualization will have a calming effect.

Breathe in slowly, deeply and mindfully through your nose while counting (slowly) to four.

Hold your breath for a moment and exhale slowly as you count to five.

Repeat several times *(and throughout the day) until you feel your body relax. (Remember this technique because it will be useful as you master all five vocal components)*

• Practice speaking, lowering your pitch as you go until you attain a comfortable level – comfortable for you and for others.

To sum up... here's what you have learned in this chapter:

• Men usually have lower pitches than women because of the gender-specific difference in length and thickness and of the vocal cords (remember: women are from Venus and men are from Mars).

• For both sexes, vibrations of the vocal cords determine the pitch.

• The pitch reveals many aspects of your (and other people's) personality - high pitch conveys anxiety and nervousness, while the lower one signals reliability, stability and emotional balance (needless to say, the latter is preferable in communicating with others).

• A monotone pitch will bore and irritate your listeners, so the message will not be passed on in an effective manner. Bringing emphasis and "life" - the rise and fall of the pitch - to the voice will bring far better results.

Please practice what you learned. In the next segment of this book, we will explore the second vocal component: **the VOLUME**.

VOLUME

The highs and lows of your voice

There is a story that U.S. President **Abraham Lincoln**, who had very long legs, was once asked by someone what the best length for the legs was. The president replied: *"Long enough to reach the ground!"*

Now, I don't know for sure whether this anecdote is true or not, but I like it nevertheless, especially since the same kind of logic could just as well apply to the volume of your voice:

It should be loud enough to convey your message, but not so loud that your dog hides under the sofa with his paws over his ears!

As you already found out in the previous chapters, a human voice conveys – through its pitch, volume, pace, tone, and rhythm – a lot of different emotions. Some nuances can be very subtle, but there is nothing subtle about the loudness or lowness of your voice.

If someone yells and screams in a casual conversation, people will likely recoil at the sound of his voice.

If, on the other hand, a person speaks very low so as to be almost inaudible, people will strain to hear him. Neither extreme is conducive to professional or social relationships.

Just as with the pitch, the volume speaks, well... volumes, about the person's feelings and the state of his or her mind. And that is why, just like all the other vocal components, it is part of the overall human communication skillset.

In this chapter, we will look at the signals the volume of our voice sends out, and list some useful techniques to control its extreme "**highs**" and "**lows**."

This is an important skill not only to a mentalizer, but also to every person who doesn't live on a deserted island. And, you'll be happy to know, the volume of your voice has absolutely **nothing** to do with the length of your legs!

Volume "on" or "off?"

A ll of us, at one time or another raise our voices. That is a natural human response to an anger-eliciting situation. By the same token, we sometimes speak very low in a whisper – to a baby, or perhaps to a loved one.

Isn't it wonderful how we can modulate our voices, adapting it to specific circumstances and emotions? Remember our great wizard **Paypee Tovary**? He reminds you that the volume of your voice is a phenomenal tool to evaluate the people around you.

Yes, when you listen to a person – you **must** concentrate and notice every slight change in their volume.

As mentalizers, we must master the ability to control our voices whenever we are surrounded by people, because the too loud or too low volume might send out the wrong kind of message.

Once you learn to recognize the meaning behind your voice's volume, you'll be better prepared to adjust it to a level that "**speaks**" positively about you, your personality, and abilities.

But before we explore this topic further, let me mention "**vocal energy**" - variations in the voice's loudness. It is most useful when you want to emphasize certain important points that you'd want your listeners to retain. There is a big difference between *"high volume,"* which is basically a raised voice that reflects anger and will scare or annoy the audience, and *"energetic voice"* that is a bit loud but conveys a message effectively and comes across to listeners as positive and inspiring.

Here's the difference between merely shouting and speaking energetically. In this clip, American civil rights activist **Dr. Martin Luther King** is giving his historic *"I Have a Dream"* speech in 1963.

Notice that he was a forceful speaker who emphasized certain parts of his speech by using a higher volume, but didn't actually shout in a way that would convey hostility.

In fact, this speech is considered to this day as one of the most inspirational messages ever given:

 7 | www.5j.biz/voice/7

Do you see what I mean by *"vocal energy?"* And do you see the **difference** between this mode of communication and screaming at the top of your lungs just because you are angry and unable to control yourself?

Be calm and in control

Now, before we go any further, let's take a moment to talk about uncontrollable anger. If you are wondering what this has to do with the volume of your voice – actually, a lot.

As mentioned above, we instinctively raise our voices when we are angry, but by doing so we send out the message to people around us that we can't control ourselves – certainly not an impressions you want to make. Therefore, it is only logical that in order to control the volume of your voice, you must learn how to rein in your anger.

Now, let me say that anger is a completely natural emotion. It only becomes a problem when it gets out of control and becomes destructive – either physically or emotionally.

So what is the solution?

I'm sure you have heard the expression: "**anger management.**" It is a set of techniques and a process of learning to recognize signs of anger, and taking positive action to calm down, so that you can express your feelings in a non-aggressive way.

Think of it as the difference between talking loudly– *yelling and screaming* – and speaking at an appropriate volume – *not too high or too low.*

You probably heard people say: "When you are angry, count to ten before speaking. If you are VERY angry, count to one hundred."

This may seem like an oversimplified bit of folk wisdom but, in fact, it is quite effective. It doesn't mean you actually have to count to ten or one hundred, but it does mean that you should take the time you need to calm down before you open your mouth!

There are several different ways and approaches to managing your anger and, therefore, the volume of your voice.

The key is to control your aggressive behavior **before** you unleash it on others and before it affects the volume of your voice, by first controlling your thoughts and emotions.

The first step is to calm down and not speak until your anger subsides. Close your eyes, take deep and cleansing breaths, and imagine a peaceful scene. Then try to rationalize your feelings by asking yourself: **"Is my anger really justified or am I overreacting?"**

If you feel it is justified, say to yourself: **"I have the right to be upset but I don't want to let my anger get out of hand and affect the way people perceive me. I will wait until I feel calmer before I speak."**

There is also a very effective technique called Emotional Intelligence, which can help you identify, understand, and manage your emotions – including anger - in a positive way.

To sum up, the best way to speak at a good vocal level is to control the *negative emotions* that influence the voice's volume.

The important of the right volume

Before we start learning a few of the mentalizer's techniques, let's first take a second and watch this short scene from the funny movie "**Austin Powers**" so we will get some perspective! Click the play button for this movie bellow:

 8 | www.5j.biz/voice/8

As already mentioned, if you raise your voice too high and sound like you are screaming, you will be perceived as an angry and aggressive person who can't control his or her emotions. You wouldn't want to get a reputation as a "**yeller**," would you?

What about someone who speaks so low, you have no idea what that person is saying?

Unless he has a sore throat or some other medical condition that prevents him from speaking at a comfortable volume, it is possible that person is very shy, unsure of him/herself, or insecure.

The same holds true for you – people will judge you and make conclusions about your personality and state of mind based on the either too high or too low volume of your voice.

So, it is only logical that you should work at giving your voice just the right volume.

Therefore, as a good mentalizer who cares about your communication skills, you would want your voice to resonate at an ear-pleasing level, in order to reflect your:

- **<u>Confidence</u>** - so you'll be able to approach people and talk them into whatever you need.

- **<u>Decisiveness</u>**, which helps in making sure people understand exactly what you expect of them.

- **<u>Good social skills</u>** - the little spice that enables you to create the relationships and attract the people you want in your life.

The good news is that you **CAN** train your voice to help you make a great impression – to...**speak well of you!**

Volume control

Let me tell you a story about my friend, **Joe**. Even since I've known him (about three years), his voice got on my nerves. He was a perfectly nice fellow, but every time he opened his mouth to say something, it sounded like a dog's bark.

Of course, Joe didn't actually bark, but he always spoke in an irritatingly **loud voice**. His volume was unchanging – *always high* – regardless of the message he was conveying.

Many times, I told him: "**Hey, Joe, keep your voice down. You sound angry and aggressive all the time.**" To which Joe always replied, "**What do you mean, 'keep it down'? I am speaking in a normal voice. And, I am certainly not angry - you know that.**"

Still, no matter how many times I pointed out to him that his voice was loud, he never adjusted his volume.

Once, when we were with a group of people, someone at the other side of the room said something funny and everyone laughed.

Everyone, that is, **except Joe**, who was completely oblivious to the joke. And then it hit me: **Joe wasn't reacting because he COULDN'T HEAR the joke.**

Yes, Joe had a hearing problem.

Once I (and he) realized this, it all became clear: Joe didn't control the volume of his voice **not because he was always angry**, but because he couldn't clearly hear himself, so he had no sense of just how loud he was. But once he got the help he needed and had a hearing aid, his voice gradually improved, and he can now adjust his volume quite well.

And this leads me to a very important point:

<u>Medical Issue Warning:</u> before you start working on adjusting the volume of your voice, there is one thing you should do... if your voice is **always** loud, then maybe the problem is in your ears.

Lots of people who have hearing loss raise their voices without meaning to or even realizing it. So the first thing you should do is have your hearing checked.

I know that there are so many elements you must master when becoming a mentalizer, including vocal aspect. Although you'll always have the great wizard Paypee Tovary helping you, I decided to collect some techniques you can use to ensure a voice that is neither too low nor too high, but just **"right:"**

Get to know your true voice: Many of us don't realize how our voice sounds to other people. So before following the exercises listed below, record your normal speaking voice. Either by the software I recommended **"The Passaggio Vocal Feedback System"** which is what I use to achieve great progress or by tape.

I study my speech patterns by recording myself when I practice different speeches, or when I want to visually see what I sound like, OR when I record others and analyze their vocal features.

I even record people on TV sometimes so I can get a better understanding of their inner feelings. Remember – you can master hearing to a great degree, but actually seeing it is always so much easier!

So go ahead and use this software, or any other tape recorder or voice recording software to record yourself at the volume you usually use. Then, as you listen to the playback - and if you use the Passaggio software – as you're *SEEING* the volume, ask yourself: **how does your voice sound to other people**?

Is it too loud, conveying anger and aggression, or maybe it is too low, sending out a message that you are timid and insecure?

Once you have a good idea of how your voice comes across, decide whether you should lower or raise your volume.

Of course, if you sound "**just right**," you are lucky!

Tips to achieving the right volume

Here are some useful tips that will help you achieve just the right volume when you speak and help you achieve better control over your own voice.

Good posture

When you were child, chances are your mother told you to sit or stand straight. Mom was right (as moms usually are!) Good posture will help you correctly position your head, neck, jaw, and abdominal muscles – all of which impact the volume of your voice.

Ask yourself: what do I sound like when I'm laying in bed? And what do I sound like when I'm trying to talk while I'm running?

You must agree that each of these positions is affecting the volume and the way you sound. So make sure your jaw is relaxed and your throat is open rather than constricted or tight.

Breathing

One of the most important keys to adjusting the volume of your voice is controlling your breathing. When I was a young boy, I would try to sing but always sang out of tune! Only when I grew older I started taking voice lessons.

I couldn't believe how much money my instructor charged me **just to tell me to breathe in and out, in and out!**

For a few weeks, I would come to my voice class and all I would do is breathe!!! I knew this was important, I just didn't know **HOW** important!

You see, it all starts and ends in the diaphragm. In the following video you will find a 3D animation that describes what exactly is the diaphragm and where it is located in your body. When we know how to use it and speak from that specific spot in our body, our voice will sound perfect and we won't run out of air as we say long sentences.

Just like in singing, in talking breathing is an important thing. Since I try to put as much information into these lessons but keeping them very short and to the point, I won't go in depth about this anatomy feature as it will take an entire book to teach, but I will ask you to practice speaking while you slowly exhale a steady stream of air.

 9 | www.5j.biz/voice/9

Of course, for best results you have to perform these exercises regularly and frequently. Each week, use The Passaggio software or your tape to record your voice again. You'll be able to see the different colors and location of your voice on the screen. Make sure you record the same paragraph each time, **not a different one**, so you can actually follow your improvements.

If it has improved, then you have been doing your homework just right and I'm happy to have you as my reader.

To end this chapter, here is a little quiz:

In a situation where you need to show someone how angry or upset you are, what will be more powerful and give you the best results:

1. Scream at them as loud as you can so they'll understand how pissed off you are.

2. Speak loud but don't scream and tell them you are very angry.

3. Speak in your normal volume but in a slow, confident manner, telling them you're upset.

4. Whisper that they did something bad and you are very sad about it.

What do you think the correct answer is? Stay tuned and you will find out my answer in the next few pages!

To sum up... Here's what you have learned in the volume topic of our book:

- **Volume is how loud you speak.** A loud volume - *yelling and screaming* - reflects anger and aggressiveness, while a low one conveys shyness and insecurity.

- There is a difference between **"vocal energy"** and **"high volume."** The former stresses certain important points of the message and fluctuates, while the latter is anger expressed through a loud voice.

- **Anger management techniques** are useful in keeping the volume of the voice at a comfortable level.

- Techniques like good posture and breathing exercises **help control the vocal volume**.

I hope you found this topic interesting and are ready for the next one, which will focus on the **tone**.

TONE

Set the tone

Have you ever wondered how many conflicts between people (and maybe even nations) are caused not by ideas, but, rather, by the tone of voice with which a particular message is conveyed?

In verbal communication, the tone of the voice is very important – it affects how people respond to us, and how we instinctively react to them. As philosopher **Friedrich Nietzsche** once said: **"We often refuse to accept an idea merely because the tone of voice in which it has been expressed is unsympathetic to us."**

He was right.

In essence, it's not only what you say, but also **HOW** you say it that determines the way your message is perceived, and whether it has a positive or negative impact on your listeners.

In previous chapters, we talked about the importance of the vocal pitch and volume in communicating with others, so you know that your voice is a very powerful tool. This is also the case with the tone – the *"right"* one will draw people to you and your ideas, while the *"wrong"* one will likely push them away. And, it goes without saying that someone who strives to be a good communicator and an effective mental analyzer **DEFINITELY** doesn't want to scare people away!

This chapter focuses on what you can do to ensure that your tone is a "**people magnet**," not "**people repeller**."

Before we start, here's a little poem (by an anonymous author), which expresses brilliantly the difference your tone of voice makes in how your message is received by others:

It's not so much what you say

As the manner in which you say it;

It's not so much the language you use

As the tone in which you convey it.

Words may be mild and fair

and the tone may pierce like a dart;

Words may be soft as the summer air

but the tone may break my heart.

Have you even thought of your tone of voice in such a way? No? Well then, you are learning a very important lesson!

Tone vs. Words

There are five elements that a great mentalizer needs to master in order to achieve the best analysis of the psychology behind what people say. Since we explained the **PITCH** and **VOLUME** in previous chapters, it is important that we understand **EXACTLY** what each component means and how we can analyze it. So just in case you are not clear on what exactly the tone of the voice is, it's a combination of the volume and the emphasis that you place on the words.

To get a clearer understanding of this concept, look at this brief video:

 10 | **www.5j.biz/voice/10**

Ok, so now you know that your tone of voice might make more of a (*positive or negative*) impression than the actual words.

To illustrate this point, let me remind you who **Dr. Albert Mehrabian** is. Born in 1939 in **Iran**, he is currently Professor Emeritus of Psychology at University of California in Los Angeles.

Dr. Mehrabian has become known by his publications on the relative importance of verbal and nonverbal messages.

His findings on inconsistent messages of feelings and attitudes have been quoted throughout human communication studies worldwide, and as we mentioned before - have also become known as the _7%-38%-55% rule_:

All our communication is divided into 55% visual communication, 38% is the voice (which we are learning about in this book), and the last 7% is the actual content.

As a guru in this field, he came up with a great example that will help us comprehend his theory.

This is how he illustrated the considerable difference the tone of voice, and most particularly the emphasis on certain words, makes in verbal communication:

<u>I</u> didn't say he borrowed my book.

I <u>DIDN'T</u> say he borrowed my book.

I didn't <u>SAY</u> he borrowed my book.

I didn't say <u>HE</u> borrowed my book.

I didn't say he <u>BORROWED</u> my book.

I didn't say he borrowed <u>MY</u> book.

I didn't say he borrowed my <u>BOOK</u>.

As you can see, the same sentence can have several meanings, depending on which word is emphasized.

The tone, therefore, can result in different innuendos, determining how others will understand – and react to – your message.

How you choose to convey your message and which words you choose to stress, will portray you either as someone who is calm and in control or someone who is prone to anger.

The French have a great saying: **"C'est le ton qui fait la musique."** Translated literally, this means, **"The tone makes (or determines) the music."**

However, what it really means is: **"It's not what you say but how you say it"** (the phrase used several times throughout this book because it really expresses, simply and succinctly, the importance of mastering your voice).

As you can see, the tone of voice is recognized as crucial in all languages, and…never gets lost in translation!

Tone up your voice

Let's look at another example, which demonstrates that oftentimes the tone "**overpowers**" the message. Here's a sentence, which, in and by itself, is neutral – neither positive nor negative:

"I don't know what you mean."

Now, let's do a little experiment. First say this sentence in an unpleasant/harsh tone of voice; then switch to a gentle tone.

Another great example will be "**Shut-up**."

We say this a lot. But scream it out loud right now with emphasis on the "**SHUT**" and *feel* what it sounds like. It's an insult to whoever hears it, and conveys anger and irritation, right?

Now say it in your normal tone of voice and **WITH A SMILE**, emphasizing the "**UP**." All of a sudden, this phrase takes on a totally different meaning. In fact, when put this way, the phrase conveys nothing negative or offensive; it's as though someone just expressed amusement at something you said: "**Shut UP, this really happened???**"

Do you see the difference that your tone of voice is making? The message itself is not changing, but its delivery determines whether you sound angry and hostile or, to the contrary, friendly and pleasant. As a mentalizer who strives to be a good communicator (as all mentalizers should be), you want to master the voice tonality not only to shape your own voice, but also so you can become better at analyzing others, and getting the **SUBTLE** messages and not only the **EXTREME** ones.

This is something that will take time to learn and master, but will become second nature to you as you practice it.

This important distinction is an asset that you must keep in mind because, as Dr. Mehrabian noted, the tone of your voice is such an important factor in the message you are conveying.

Think about it: a large part of what comes out of your mouth and lands in someone's ears determines how they perceive you. And, of course, this also applies to how you judge other people by their tone.

Your job is to listen to the way people are speaking out their messages. You must concentrate on the pitch and volume, as you learned in the previous chapters, and then note the subtle emphasis they are putting on different words in their sentences. This will allow you to analyze their thoughts and true meanings.

Now, you can't do anything about how others communicate, but you can certainly manage your own tone. This is another crucial element for a mentalizer when it comes to controlling and conveying your messages to others.

Remember, the stronger your speaking abilities, the easier it'll become to influence the public the way **YOU** want to do it – by motivating and inspiring them in a **POSITIVE** manner.

Coach your voice!

Obviously, we are not born into this world with excellent vocal skills – in fact, the only ability we have at the beginning of our lives is to cry **LOUD** when we are hungry! That's a reflex, rather than a learned behavior. It is only later in life that we are able to learn and develop our voices in the art form of communicating effectively and successfully.

Beyond the same voice exercises you do to improve your pitch and volume (controlling your posture as well as abdomen, chest and throat muscles), you can also go a long way toward improving your tone by being aware and conscious.

Let me explain. The tone, just like the pitch and volume, is influenced by our emotions. So if you are nervous, tense, or angry, the best approach is to say nothing until you have the time to chill out .

Remember when, in the previous chapter, I talked about anger management? Those tips apply just as well to tone control and, for that matter, control of all the vocal components.

Words, once spoken, can't be taken back.

That's why you should assess your emotional state before you speak out; this way you will not only avoid hurting someone's feelings, but will also develop the ability to control yourself in any given situation so you always appear to be cool and collected – in other words, calm and dignified, which is just the way a mentalizer should be!

Much depends on what your position in life is – whether you're a student, a teacher, a businessperson, or in a certain relationship where you want to use your tone (and other vocal components) to influence the person you're with.

Think of the possibilities and the power you posses.

Let's look at a few more examples:

If you're a teacher and you say to a student: "**You think you know**," your tone will decide whether you encourage the student to give you an answer, or you insult her by making her think you don't believe in her. In other words, depending on *how* you say it, this phrase may come across as sarcastic and nasty (not the way a teacher should be!) or encouraging.

Try it now - say: You **THINK** you know! Say it in an insulting tone so you'll hear what it sounds like. Doesn't it come across in a demeaning, *"you-are-really-stupid"* kind of way? Now say: "You think you **KNOW**?" In contrast to the previous example, this conveys your interest in what the student has to say, and encourages her to share her view.

What if you are a student who needs to present something in the classroom? You would like to know how the tone will impact your listeners so you'll be able to control it rather than let it control you!

Before speaking, always ask yourself what you want to achieve and what your listeners need to remember – what is the final goal of your presentation – and use your tonality to achieve it.

Here is a useful tip:

No matter what your position in life is, before you want to say something meaningful – write it down.

Now, mark with a marker, or an underline, the "key" words that are important in your message. Once you do this, write under each marked word a feeling you want to convey. Then, practice speaking it with the right tonality (as well as pitch and volume) that matches the emotion you want the specific words to express.

Think of feelings such as **"sad," "excited," "aggravated," "fulfilled," "angry," "enthralled," "disgusted," "happy,"** etc…

I have something I must show you. And to be honest, it was hard for me to decide in which chapter to show it to you – because it's such a beautiful and strong scene from a TV show that shows a phenomenal range of emotions: anger, fear, sadness, joy, contempt, compassion - all within three minutes!

I thought to myself that I should be showing it to you only in the last voice lesson, but then I realized that it can give you a great overview of what we are learning. Also, you'll be able to come back to this video and watch it again and again, so you'll be able to practice your analysis of how people convey their feelings.

This scene is considered a master class for any aspiring actor since **James Gandolfini**, the star of the long-running TV show, "**The Sopranos**," really nailed it. So, without further ado, here's the episode 1×11 entitled *"Nobody Knows Anything:"*

11 | www.5j.biz/voice/11

What did we learn?

In the previous chapters, you've learned about the volume of your voice. The question I asked was: "**In a situation where you need to show someone how angry or upset you are, what will be more powerful and give you the best results:**"

1. Scream at them as loud as you can so they'll understand how pissed off you are.

2. Speak loud but don't scream and tell them you are very angry.

3. Speak in your normal volume but in a slow, confident manner, telling them you're upset.

4. Whisper that they did something bad and you are very sad about it.

When I lecture or perform in different places around the world, I always use this example.

What I usually do is simply ask it and then most of them say: **number 2.** But then, to make my point clearer, I bring four people on stage and let each one of them read from a scripted paper that also gives them instructions of how to *"perform"* it. Then I ask my audience members again which person has the strongest effect on them... What do you think their answer is?

Well, their new answer is option number 3.

Why?

When you're speaking loud or screaming, it means that you have lost control or that you're in a certain mindset that might be temporary. Usually, people don't scream or talk loud *all the time*, right? So when you shout at someone, they will automatically think to themselves **"Ok, I should let this pass and everything will be alright,"** without actually realizing they did something wrong.

HOWEVER, when you speak in your normal voice but in a slow and confident matter you are actually making them understand that something is really wrong and that you're not experiencing a temporary anger that will soon pass... The tone of your voice must be controlled by you all the time.

To sum up...

Here's what you have learned so far:

• Tone is the combination of the **volume**, the **pitch** and the **emphasis** that you place on the words.

• The tone determines how your message is received by others.

- Any sentence can have a different meaning and convey a different mood (positive or negative), depending on which words are emphasized.

- Awareness and consciousness of the way the tone can impact your speech is therefore essential in communicating with others.

I hope you found this topic to be interesting and informative. By the time we finish exploring all there is to know about the voice, you will become a vocal expert! So stay tuned for the next topic – **the pace**.

In the meantime, stop for a second and think of a sentence that you said in the past but its meaning wasn't conveyed the way you wanted to - people understood it differently. Now that you have a better understanding of the vocal pitch, volume, and tone, how would you convey this message differently?

ce

pace

PACE

Pace yourself!

Simply put, the pace of voice is the speed with which somebody speaks. Have you ever listened to someone who spoke so fast, you not only couldn't catch a word he or she was saying, but got a headache from trying to follow their words?

Or maybe someone spoke so slllooooowwwwllllly, you couldn't focus on the message because the pace of the voice was putting you to sleep?

Take a look at these two videos:

 12 | www.5j.biz/voice/12

 13 | www.5j.biz/voice/13

The first one is an example of real fast talk (granted, it is exaggerated and not something you encounter every day, but only by showing you the 'extreme' you'll be able to comprehend what I'm trying to convey).

The second video features a speaker who takes his time explaining a point that could be delivered much quicker.

So which of the two – fast talk or the slow one – is a better communication tool?

The answer is: **NEITHER!** The first one **agitates** and the second one **bores**, and neither of them conveys the message as effectively as he would with a steady pace.

I myself have been subjected to presentations that were either too fast or too slow, and in each case I wanted to go to the speaker and say, "**Hey, man, let me teach you a thing or two about pacing!**"

The fact is that many people (and perhaps you are one of them?) don't know how to pace their speech. Or maybe you didn't even realize that the pace makes a huge difference in how your message is received by your listeners.

Some people also speak very fast because they lack confidence. Like, when someone is brought on stage and they are supposed to say something but because they are so tense, they speak very fast and "*swallow*" their words, which makes it hard to understand what they are saying and you can very easily tell how stressed they are.

In fact, when most people are put in the spotlight - even in a harmless conversation where all of a sudden you shoot an intimate question at them, or try to tell them they are lying - they will start talking fast or stutter in a way that will seem as if they are "*losing it.*"

Do you know that feeling? You probably saw it happen many times with your own friends or even experienced it yourself.

In my own work as a mentalizer, I am aware of the importance of pacing my voice so it is **"just right"** – not painfully slow or irritatingly fast. By the same token, I have also learned all about the proper pitch, volume, tone, and rhythm – all the components discussed in this book.

But you don't have to be a professional mentalizer and perform on stages around the world to adapt a pleasant, ear-pleasing pace.

As you know by now, body language (both verbal and nonverbal) is a reflection of **your personality**, which is why you should train yourself to make a great impression – consciously. If you rely only on your subconscious responses, you will likely make some mistakes in the way you put yourself *"out there"* for other people to see and judge.

As everything else outlined in this book, achieving your goals is within your reach – as long as you practice diligently all the outlined steps and techniques.

This is what scientists tell us...

In 2011, a research team from the **University of Michigan** in the United States investigated the best way to communicate so that the message falls on receptive ears– in other words, that it is conveyed clearly and elicits positive response from the listeners.

Not surprisingly, these researchers found that the ideal style of speech is not too fast and not too slow, steady rather than overly animated, and punctuated with frequent, short pauses.

Speakers who deliver their messages *too slowly* or *too fast* aren't as effective at getting people to listen to them, the study found. That's because people who talk fast tend to be seen as **untrustworthy**, while those who speak too slowly are usually perceived as **slow-witted** or overly **pedantic – finicky** and **fussy**.

Also, when listening to a slow speaker, people may think: **"Why is he talking to us so slowly? Does he think we are idiots???"** Right? I'm sure you've had that feeling before.

The researchers also reported that speakers who are overly animated and excitable use lots of pitch variation in their voices, and that's not a good thing either.

So what kind of speakers got the best feedback?

Predictably, those with an even-keeled, steady, and well-paced voice have the best chance of making a great impression on their listeners, the study reported.

Their words – whether sales pitches or inspirational messages – were **"heard"** and **"received"** clearly and effectively by their audiences, which is what good communication is all about and that is exactly what you are aiming for.

Connect with your listeners

In the previous chapter, we spoke about the tone of the voice and how different emphasis on different words gives us a different meaning for the same sentence. When I introduced you to the great wizard Paypee Tovary, I thought to myself that *Pay* (the beginning of the name) which stands for *PACE*, should be the first thing we put our mind to when we listen to someone – or speak ourselves.

When we first analyze someone's speech, we call up Paypee Tovary, and we concentrate first on the *PACE* of their voice. So let's learn how to do it, and why it is so important.

Most people tend to talk too fast – so called *motormouths* – making it difficult to *"hang on"* to their every word, or, for that matter, their general message, as demonstrated in the above video featuring a fast talking auctioneer. If that is how you communicate as well, **now is the time to change it**.

Obviously, this is a very bad habit, for several reasons. First, whatever it is that you are trying to convey –whether talking to a colleague, client, friend, or family member – will not be absorbed by the other party. Secondly, as mentioned in previous chapters, the way you speak reflects your emotional state, and fast talk often means that you are stressed out and excitable, rather than calm and in control of yourself.

What about speaking too slowly?

This is less common than high-speed talk, but it also sends out a message – that you are shy, insecure, and unsure of yourself.

A mentalizer must pay attention to the pace because it is indicative of the speaker's mental and emotional state. When someone slows down or is getting faster as he or she speaks, we use the term "**NORMING**" because it is the way we can evaluate a person's thoughts or feelings.

What exactly is norming?

It is a technique that analyzes body language and non-verbal cues in contrast to how a person responds normally to situations. A mentalizer uses this approach to unlock the secrets of the mind.

So basically, when we listen to a person, we will try to "**normalize**" their speech pattern *before* we draw conclusions about the way they speak.

If they speak **fast**, we will note the times when they slow down, as it will give us a clue to what they are thinking. If they talk **slowly** and suddenly go faster – it means something is happening in their head!

How should a mentalizer speak?

The correct answer is "**JUST RIGHT**" – neither too fast nor too slow. Listen to a newsreader on TV or a professional speaker to get the idea of the comfortable and desirable pacing, and how effective it is in commanding the listeners' attention and getting your messages across.

Slow down here; we know that choosing the moderate approach is always better because it makes sense, right? You don't have to be a master mental analyzer to know you shouldn't scream or whisper when you talk, that you shouldn't talk too fast or too slow; we simply know that being **"in between"** is always the right way to go.

However, having a good pace doesn't mean you should not vary it while you speak. After all, you don't want to sound like a robot (remember what we said in the previous chapter about a monotone voice?)

Depending on the type of message you are communicating, some display of emotion, and therefore either faster or slower pace, may be acceptable – as long as it changes and fluctuates within the speech as needed and is not constantly too fast or slow.

Those of us who often perform in front of an audience have learned this, and you can too. This is called **"elocution"** – clear and expressive speech.

The Vocal Axis

Now is a good time to introduce you to the concept "**Vocal Axis**." If you take its literal definition, axis means *"an imaginary line to which various elements are referred for measurement or symmetry."*

How does this relate to the voice?

Think of the voice as running along an axis, with extremes such as loud vs. low and slow vs. fast. Being in the "**middle**" of this axis is the right approach when we try to communicate, **but it also enables us to mentally analyze people in front of us**.

Yes, it sounds overwhelming at first when I tell my students that they will be able to hear someone and **immediately** dissect their voice into small pieces and analyze it. But now, as we learn the process step by step, it all should make sense to you!

We are learning how to take each sentence someone says and analyze it by dissecting it into the five elements of the voice (pace, pitch, tone, volume and rhythm), and the next step is to put each one of these aspects on our analyzing axis.

This means that we will determine where on this axis the person is located in each one of these vocal aspects, thus giving us a unique "**view**" of this person's thoughts and overall emotional state. **Does it start to make sense to you now? Isn't it so exciting?**

By the time you finish reading this book **AND PRACTICING IT** you'll know how to understand each element and how the location of this element on the *vocal axis* reflects the personality of the person talking to you at that specific moment.

And the most phenomenal thing about this experience is that you will soon find out that **NO ONE** is the same!

Just as each of us has his or her own and unique set of fingerprints, we all have a different type of a voice pattern as well.

Why is this happening?

Because each person has a whole different personality, which is reflected in the way he expresses his ideas and feelings. Of course, most listeners are not able to "**catch**" these subtleties, but you, who master the mentalizer's tools, can!

Remember that when it comes to **YOU**, you must try to be as balanced as possible and this is why I keep orienting you to the middle approach of speaking "**just right**." Being in the middle, or "**moderate**" and "**controlled**" rather than extreme, is never wrong – whether in voice quality or life in general.

The 'JUST RIGHT' Approach

"You keep telling me to speak 'Just Right!' Why is it so important to focus and concentrate on the way we speak all the time? It's exhausting."

This is what most of my students tell me when they hear my lectures or read my books. We understand that we are affecting the person we talk to in so many ways. When we talk at a high and intense volume, or very fast, our listeners will get defensive and worried because we use our voice in an unbalanced way that changes the mood of the person in front of us.

If, for instance, a young lady speaks to a man in a slow pace with a low volume - he will not be able to concentrate and be himself.

He will feel aroused or sexually interested, because her speech pattern is located on the **"sexual"** spot in the *voice axis*.

Hey, I am just giving you an example!

You understand that if I need to read someone and I talk in a way, which is different than the *"flat 0 axis"* manner, I am changing the way the person in front of me will react to me.

I hope this makes sense to you.

So the answer is to try and be as **"middle-ground"** as we can - to speak **"just right."**

By doing this, we aren't **"projecting"** ourselves on the listeners and we can truly see what their *REAL* deep thoughts and emotions are because we are not swaying them one way or another – not putting any expectations on them regarding how they should respond to us.

We are totally neutral, and it's up to the listeners to **"reveal"** themselves to us.

I hope I made it clear enough for you to understand the importance of keeping your voice in the middle of the axis.

Keeping up the pace

There are some relatively simple tricks to mastering your pace but, as in all the other lessons, you must practice and exercise. If you speak too quickly, you must first find some **"de-stressors"** that work for you.

Remember: if you speak while nervous or anxious, your pace might speed up. Try any or all of these techniques, or find one that works best for you:

Sit comfortably, close your eyes and take slow, deep breaths. If you really concentrate and repeat this several times, you will feel the tension leave your body.

Imagine being a super hero. No one can harm you in any way. In fact, you are the ruler of the universe and you control everyone.

By seeing this vision you will be able to feel the power. Imagine what a super hero, who is the ruler of the planet, sounds like when he talks:

A balanced, clear and powerful way of speaking.

In addition to breathing, you might benefit from an **NLP** (*Neuro-lingistic Programming*) technique. In NLP, anchors are stimuli – usually a gesture, touch, or sound – that condition your mind to trigger positive responses to achieve an emotional state you want.

So by all means, try this technique when you need to chase nervousness and anxiety away. By programming yourself using an anchor to slow down, you'll be able to use these stimuli every single time your voice pacing starts running wild.

As an example, try creating a fun anchor of tapping with the tip of your index finger on the tip of your thumb three times in a row.

Tap-tap-tap.

Program yourself to slow down using this anchoring. So when you're chatting with someone important and you feel that you're over speeding, simply perform this anchoring technique and see how your pace immediately goes down.

Use this while in interviews, an important business meeting, a weekly get-together with the boss, or any other interaction.

Once you are sufficiently relaxed, get to the voice pacing exercise. One approach that has proven to be successful for a lot of people is imagining a long sentence without any punctuation. Then, visualize the same phrase with the commas and semi-colons – these are your "**markers**" where a pause, intake of breath, or a slower pace should occur. Again, practice this technique repeatedly, until you can hear your pace normalizing.

Here's an example. Say this sentence:

"I don't want to see this movie it is too violent I don't like violence I prefer romantic films."

Now let's repeat it, slowing down slightly where you see punctuation:

"I don't want to see this movie, it is too violent. I don't like violence; I prefer romantic films."

Do you see how punctuation slows down the way you say this sentence? Not dramatically, but just enough to make it smoother and well paced?

Now, what should you do if your pace is too slow and everyone around you is yawning or falling asleep?

Choose a page from a book or a newspaper and read it out loud at your usual snail-pace speed. Then, if it took you, say, five minutes to get through the text, give yourself three or four minutes and try again, until you reach a comfortable speed.

This exercise is best done with another person present, who can judge your speed and provide feedback. You can also record yourself practicing and get someone you trust to assess your progress.

Ok, let's move on to some practical analysis of vocal pace. Say we want to show self-confidence. Our pace will be slow and confident, while stressing the words we want emphasized using the **tone** of our voice.

But what if you are is not so confident and speak at a fast pace, trying to convey the confidence that you don't really have.

Imagine yourself walking into a job interview. Usually you would try and speak in a fast pace in order to "*show off*" your knowledge. "**Yes sir, I know how this works as I had performed this task many times in the past and I can assure you that if you hire me you will not be disappointed yaba yaba yaba...**" Say this line quickly and you'll know exactly what I mean.

In a way, when we speak at a balanced pace – not too fast and not too slow – it gives us plenty of time to think about what we are about to say (or at least the concept of what we want to convey), and we can choose the right pacing, as well as the other components of our speech, in order to **bring out the best of us**.

Let's take a look at this short scene from "Breaking Bad" so we can see this concept what in action:

 14 | www.5j.biz/voice/14

We have a guy who needs a badass next to him to achieve his goal. The pacing of his voice is fast and he barely stops to breathe when he speaks. He is connecting sentences and ideas very fast, and only stops to get **Huell** to support him.

Then we have Huell, who is performing the intimidating pose exactly like I spoke about before - he speaks slowly and puts emphasis on certain words. So there you have it.

The pace of your voice will determine how powerful you are. Period.

So now we studied the first four elements of the human voice –the Pitch, the Volume, the Tone and the Pace. We are only missing the Ry from our wizard Paypee Tovary – which is the **rhythm** – our next chapter.

I hope you were able to memorize his name by now, so every time you hear someone you want to analyze you stop for a second, remember Paypee Tovary, and immediately start analyzing their voice. In the meantime, please practice what you have just learned in this chapter. I have a few exercises to help you implement this new information:

Take one day this week and decide that it'll be your *"fast pace day."* Speak very fast that day. At work, with your family, in school, wherever you are – just speak fast. Think about what you want to say, and then say it as fast as possible. Not in a comic way, but in a normal fast pace. Then choose a *"slow pace day"* and **ONLY** speak slowly to everyone you come in contact with.

After every conversation, and at the end of each day, evaluate your feelings and what you've learned from this process. Ask yourself these questions:

What was people's response to me?

How did they interact with me?

Did they look at me differently?

Did they understand me better?

Were they upset with me?

Overall, did the fact that I was speaking fast or slow make me feel different – better or worse?

Once you test this in your daily life, you start realizing the importance of pace and how it affects you or others. When you grasp this concept, it'll be easier for you to understand the psychology behind it. Soon, when you'll hear others speak fast or slow in certain times or certain sentences, you'll be able to pinpoint what's going on in their mind at that particular time!

To sum up...

Here's what you have learned in the *pace topic*:

• Pace is the speed with which somebody speaks.

• Speaking too quickly will portray you as stressed and excitable, rather than someone who is in control of him/herself and therefore credible and reliable.

• The pace that is too slow signals insecurity and lack of confidence.

• Techniques like norming, NLP, relaxation, deep breathing, and imagery can help control the pace, so that it is neither too slow nor too fast.

• The *voice-axis* is the secret to analyzing each person's state of mind in any given moment.

RHYTHM

Get Rhythm!

In previous chapters, we talked about all the essential vocal components as parts of the larger concept of human communication. You learned how important pitch, volume, tone, and pace are in communicating effectively, and how to master the art of controlling all these key vocal elements.

In this chapter, we will explore the fifth component – **the rhythm**.

Now, I bet that if someone mentions the word *"rhythm"* to you, the first thought you have is **"music,"** and not the spoken word.

True, rhythm is commonly associated with different musical genres, and quite a few songs had been written about it – *"Get Rhythm"* and *"Fascinating Rhythm,"* among others.

But the fact is that rhythm is also an integral part of our speech patterns. Maybe that's why melodious tones are sometimes referred to as **"singing voices"**.

People – no matter where they live or what language they speak, -love to listen to a speech that exhibits rhythmic patterns because it is not only **"easy"** on their ears, but also more interesting.

Of course, the more interesting and well delivered the speech is, the more of a positive impact it will make on your listeners – whether you are speaking to a small group or a huge audience.

In this chapter we will also briefly sum up the four other vocal components we talked about before, just so that you have a global view of the things you've learned – and should know by now (*I am assuming you've been practicing and exercising!*)

And this is another thing you hopefully learned:

Even though you may not have given your voice much thought or attention in the past, now you know it is a very essential communication tool.

As American writer **F. Scott Fitzgerald** put it in his famous novel, *The Great Gatsby*: **"The exhilarating ripple of her voice was a wild tonic in the rain."**

What he meant to convey was not just that the book's heroine, **Daisy**, had a beautiful voice, but also that it had a powerful effect on the people she spoke to.

That's what good oral communication is all about and this is exactly what we are learning in these chapters!

Shape up your voice

In case you are not sure what "**rhythm**" means, it is the evenness or unevenness of the rate of speech. It is determined by tempo variations and "**word stress**" – the way we emphasize certain words when we speak. It can also be defined as "**the patterns of stress and intonation in a spoken language**."

If you really listen carefully to how others talk, or become conscious of your own speech, you will realize that most of us speak at our own individual rhythms. Just like the pitch, volume, tone, and pace, the rhythm of the voice reveals the speaker's mindset, emotional state, and attitude.

It is, in a way, a combination of all the other four elements and it is also the reason why I chose it to be the final touch in the overall analysis. This is why the Ry is being called last when using the Paypee TovaRY mnemonic system.

If you combine all the vocal components, your listeners will get a pretty good picture of what your thoughts and feelings are, which is a compelling reason to whip your voice into the best possible shape.

If you can't control your pitch, volume, tone, pace, and rhythm, you may be perceived as hostile and angry, or anxious and insecure – certainly not the best way towards achieving effective communication.

If, on the other hand, you practice the techniques outlined in previous chapters, such as relaxation, breathing, muscle control, etc., you will train your voice to portray you as someone who is reliable, credible, and masterful – just the way a mentalizer and an excellent communicator should be!

In the previous chapter, I asked you to do a fun exercise: to choose a '*fast pace*' day and a '*slow pace*' day and see how people react to you in each of these two circumstances.

I told you to speak very fast on the fast pace day, and answer questions very fast. Did you notice what effect it had on the people you were talking to?

And when you were speaking slooooowly, and taking your time to put your thoughts out there (not in a comical way but really as if you were considering every word you said), what effect did that behavior have on the people around you?

I'm sure you've noticed the difference in the way people were reacting to you!

This is due to the fact that every aspect of our voice critically affects the way we are being perceived, consciously and non-consciously.

Different rhythm different message

You may not have realized until now how a voice rhythm can determine the kind of message you want to convey. Have a look at this sentence: *"I have to go to work."* Now, let's see how different emphasis on different words, the aforementioned **"word stress"**, changes the meaning of what you want to convey.

<u>I</u> - have to go to work. The stress on the "I" means that while your *listener* can go to a party or otherwise enjoy himself, *you* have to go to work.

I - <u>*have to*</u> - go to work. Here, you are saying that you have no choice – you *MUST* go to work, rather than engage in other activities.

I have to go to - <u>*work*</u>. This means that no – you can't go to a party or do any other activity, because you have to **work**.

<u>I</u> - have to go to - <u>*work*</u>. Here you are telling a person who is enticing you to goof off and keep her company that, even though she can have some leisure time, <u>you can't</u> – you must live up to your obligations and go to work.

This is just one example, but obviously, rhythm or word stress and word emphasis plays a significant role in our speech patterns. You may not have realized this before, since you were doing it subconsciously, but now that you are aware of the importance of a rhythmic voice, you will use it to your best advantage.

Lost in translation?

Now, a very important point when talking about the rhythm, as well as the four other vocal components, is that each language has its particular – and sometimes peculiar – rhythm. For example, in **English**, sentences are spoken with varying bursts of speed, long or short pauses, and intonation breaks. **Americans** speak with a melody, almost like singing a song. If an American will try to speak in a monotonous rhythm he will sound bizarre! Or maybe he will sound **British**!

Another example is that **French, Italian, Hebrew** and some **London** speakers all omit the "*h*" sound in English speech. Obviously, other languages have their own structural characteristics; after all, English doesn't sound anything like French, Japanese or Hebrew.

I speak Hebrew and English. When I switch over to English, I completely change my rhythm so I won't have a thick Israeli accent.

In Hebrew, we speak much slower than in English. Maybe one day I'll record myself for you so you'll be able to hear what I sound like when I talk with a thick Israeli accent! It's quite funny.

But as I moved to the **USA** and wanted to perform and appear on TV and on stages around the country, it was very important to me to sound as American as possible just so people would understand me perfectly. It would be pretty weird going on stage on **Broadway** and speaking with a thick accent when no one can understand you...

When I realized how important my accent was, I hired **Sam Schwat** – New York's premiere speech pathologist, who simply reshapes the way you speak completely.

In his studio, he taught all the greatest actors how to sound the way they wanted: **Robert De Niro, Leonardo DeCaprio, Julia Roberts** and plenty of others chose him for his effective speech method.

The Sam Shwat Method trains people to take control of their speech. By teaching me to self-monitor and self-correct, it gave me the tools to change, in just a few months, my Israeli speech habits for a lifetime. I still have the tape recordings of all the sessions I had there... I didn't have much money then, and the price was really high at the time but I knew I was making a good investment!

As a mentalizer, these lessons gave me so much more information than you can imagine. Although the experts in this center believe they teach people how to speak in the right rhythm, they also give clients an incredible inside look at the way people think!

Most of the material I spoke about in the past four lessons came to me while spending hours in this little studio in Manhattan's Union Square!

So, yes, I'm saving you lots of money by summing it all up in this book!

I guess that I was lucky to relocate to New York City. It is one place that simply has everything, and that includes the many different cultures! So I could just sit in the subway, on my way home, and listen to the way people spoke whether they sat to my right, left or in front of me!

In fact, I used to put on my earphones but **the music wasn't even playing!** That way people who saw me felt very comfortable talking next to me – they thought I'm too busy listening to some music! And you should know by now that *people watching*, or in our case *'people hearing'*, is a phenomenal exercise for every aspiring mentalizer! You just learn so much!

And I learned.

First, I learned to recognize the different accents. If you had a chance to see one of my shows in New York, you know I can tell so much about a person right after they say their first line!

Just by listening to their accent AND rhythm you can tell where they come from. Even languages that are part of the same group (for example, Italian and Spanish) often have different tempos, intonations, and rates of speed. These variations in the way people express themselves both verbally and non-verbally are not only linguistic, but also cultural.

Take, for example, Hebrew, my mother tongue, and French. They sound similar to someone who doesn't know how to speak either language, except for one main thing: French people finish their sentence in a **high pitch** (*going up*) while Israelis finish their sentence in a **low pitch** (*going down*). Does this mean that the French are optimistic people and Israelis are not? I don't know whether it's true or not, but that might be a topic for another book!

All these factors should be taken into account when trying to interpret someone's speech patterns and body language. This is where cultural sensitivity kicks in.

For instance, some people, like the Japanese, have their own way of "**reading**" body language, which is not consistent with the way people in the West do it. So the thing to keep in mind is to customize your vocal components to your language and culture. If, like me, you speak more than one language, then there is no way around it – **master the nuances of each one!**

Here's a really fun video that will show you **EXACTLY** what I am talking about. Actor **Nick Foti**, is showing his skills with accents. He actually speaks English with 35 different accents!

Here is the list of accents he does in the video (and I want you to really concentrate on the last ones from the far away countries so you'll be able to notice how the rhythm changes dramatically!):

- **General American**
- **New York City/North Jersey**
- **Philadelphia/South Jersey**
- **Boston**
- **Southern American**
- **Redneck**
- **Midwestern**
- **Southwestern**

- California Surfer
- California Valley Girl
- Urban American Girl
- Transatlantic 1940s
- 1940s Gangster
- Canadian
- Mexican
- Jamaican
- Irish
- English
- Medieval English
- Cockney English
- Australian
- French
- German
- Russian
- Italian
- Spanish
- Filipino
- Mandarin Chinese
- Cantonese Chinese
- Japanese
- Korean
- Vietnamese
- Arabian
- Indian
- Kenyan

15 | **www.5j.biz/voice/15**

To sum up this and four previous lessons, remember that:

• **Pitch** is the voice **range**.

• **Volume** is the **loudness or lowness** of your voice.

• **Tone** a combination of **volume** and **emphasis** you place on words.

• **Pace** is the **speed** with which you speak.

• **Rhythm** means **evenness** or **unevenness** – the "*tempo*" that is being created by your voice; where all the elements are coming together.

Individually, they paint only a partial picture of your inner emotional and mental state, but **combined together** on the *voice-axis*, and used in conjunction with non-verbal body language, they are powerful indicators of moods and feelings, which you – and others – convey while speaking.

Once you become proficient in all of these parts of the puzzle, you will be able to decipher ideas, meanings, and emotions in what people are telling you.

And, if you master all these components yourself, you will learn to communicate the way mentalizers like myself do: create anticipation, build suspense, and influence your listeners, so that they hang on to your every word and gesture.

How great it that?

Practice analyzing the 5 elements

I want you to really practice these elements of the voice, and I want to make it easier for you. So I have another fun video to share with you, and the reason why I love it so much is because of the different vocal styles packed into it in less than 5 minutes!

I want you to remember the five components of the speech as you watch this phenomenal appearance by **Jared M. Gordon**! Even when he is imitating a cartoon, you can learn so much about the character he is referring to simply by hearing one line!

This is a great practice for you: Simply watch this video five times. Yes, **FIVE times.** But each time I want you to pay attention to a different vocal component.

So basically, first time simply watch it and pay attention to the *pacing* of his words so you'll see how **fast** he speaks when he imitates **Lisa Simpson** and how **slow** when he imitates **Homer Simpson**; second time concentrate on the *pitch* so you'll notice the high pitch for Lisa and than a low one for Homer; then concentrate on the *tone*, the *volume* and the *rhythm*. Soon you'll get much better at analyzing different sounds and voices.

You'll know how to tell which characteristics each person has simply by listening to one sentence!

16 | www.5j.biz/voice/16

So there it is. Hopefully, you were practicing every single one of the past five chapters and by now you mastered the secret that the wizard Paypee Tovary has taught you.

You realize now that you don't have to meet someone in person in order to analyze them. Many times you will be able to interpret someone's feelings and thoughts simply by listening to the way they sound over the phone, or on the radio.

Or let's take a look at another example: you're a worried parent and you sit in the living room while your kids are in the next room. You can't see them but you can hear them. You use your mentalizer abilities to analyze their current mood or how stressed they are simply by hearing their voices as they talk to each other.

Many times you don't even have to listen to the words, just to their pace, pitch, tone, volume and rhythm!

And, of course, you can use all these techniques yourself while communicating with others. If you are diligent about it, you will see how well you'll be able to "**spread**" your ideas.

This is really powerful stuff, my friends. The voice of the person is his **output to the world**. You can learn so much from analyzing someone's body language and non-verbal behavior, but only once they open their mouth is when you get the **COMPLETE** picture.

Your homework is to analyze as many people as you can! And you don't even have to actually interact with them: if you're at a coffee shop, simply listen to the people at the table next to you. Analyze them based on their voice and even draw a *voice-axis* five times on a napkin (one for each vocal component) and place "0" line in the middle. Then simply place a little mark on the location of each vocal attribute you hear!

If you're on the bus or train, analyze the voice of other passengers. Even if you're just walking in the street and someone is talking on the phone in front of you, walk a little faster until you're closer and listen to the way they talk.

Ask yourself the following questions:

- *Who are they talking to? Their friend? Their spouse?*

- *Is it a serious matter? Is it a small talk?*

- *Are they in love? Is he angry?*

- *And any other question you can come up with!*

Don't worry – you'll know! If you've practiced all the lessons so far, your mind should be wide open to discover what these people are thinking and get a glimpse into their world based on a few words they say!

Please spend some time familiarizing yourself with all that was taught in this book.

Don't just read it "**blindly**," without paying careful attention to each and every thing I taught you. As you already know from a previous chapter, being able to focus, be attentive, and analyze all that you hear are the "**secret**" tools to better communication.

Ok, they were secret before you started this book because, I bet, you never really paid conscious attention to them. Now, they are no longer shrouded in mystery!

Miles to go...

Before we move on to the **BONUS** chapter, I'd like you to do an exercise. the reason I am suggesting it is because it will help you see how well you have assimilated all the concepts explained in this book and how effectively you can put them into practice.

Also, it will help you understand, in practice rather than just theory, what a big difference the five elements – pitch, tone, volume, pace, and rhythm – will make in your verbal communication.

Are you ready? Great, let's go.

If you have never read the works by **Robert Frost**, the preeminent American poet who penned such well-known poems as "**The Road Not Taken**," I recommend that you do, because they are wonderful.

But for this exercise, I chose his poem titled "**Stopping by Woods on a Snowy Evening**."

Here it is:

Whose woods these are I think I know.
His house is in the village, though;
He will not see me stopping here
To watch his woods fill up with snow.

My little horse must think it queer
To stop without a farmhouse near
Between the woods and frozen lake
The darkest evening of the year.

He gives his harness bells a shake
To ask if there is some mistake.
The only other sound's the sweep
Of easy wind and downy flake.

The woods are lovely, dark, and deep,
But I have promises to keep,
And miles to go before I sleep,
And miles to go before I sleep.

Now, I'd like you to read this poem out loud, using all the techniques you have learned as far as pitch, tone, volume, pace, and rhythm are concerned.

First do one component at a time, and then use all of them together – it may not be easy to start with, but if you are conscious and aware of each and every element, you will do just fine. Don't give up if at first you don't succeed – try again!

Here's one rendition of this poem:

17 | www.5j.biz/voice/17

Note the reciter's changing pitch, tone, volume, pace, and rhythm, which bring **"life"** to this poem.

Now, this doesn't mean that you have to recite it exactly the same way – as you probably know, there are no rules in art and you should read it out the way you **"feel"** it, as long as you are careful to maintain the right pitch, tone, volume, pace, and rhythm, and not just blurt it out in a rapid and flat voice.

Let's take, for example, the last two lines of the poem, *"And miles to go before I sleep."* You can stress the word **"miles"** or **"go"** – the first one expressing the long distance still to be traveled, while the second emphasis is on the action....**do you see what I mean?**

Terrific! This means you've been **LISTENING, FOCUSING** and **PAYING ATTENTION** to everything in this book. **I am one satisfied teacher!**

In the next, **BONUS** chapter, I will share with you some very pertinent information and tips about being a better communicator by using the five vocal components, as well as other techniques, while you speak – whether to an audience or just a few people.

The purpose of effective communication is to make sure that your ideas are successfully transmitted to and received by the people on whom you want to make an impact. It is a very useful skill, which can improve your life, **as well as the lives of others**.

BONUS
CHAPTER

Bonus chapter:
Improving your communication

"**A word, well spoken, can influence the minds and thoughts of the whole mankind.**"

~Anonymous

Dear friends, now that you have learned about the importance of the voice, I'd like to share with you information about effective speaking – whether you are interacting with a small group of people or an audience of hundreds.

The things written in this chapter come from the knowledge and experience drawn from many years of performing and influencing thousands of people in my shows on stages around the world or on primetime TV in the biggest networks.

Unless you live on a deserted island, you must learn the best communication skills.

Simply put, human communication is the act of transferring information from one person to another. Now, notice that I said "**human**" communication, but there is a vast body of evidence indicating that all living creatures have their own unique style of "**talking**" and responding to each other.

In fact, animals big and small communicate through vocalizations inherent to their species – the chirping of birds, barking of dogs, and so on.

Of course, we are going to focus only on human communication although, as you know, there are people who specialize in understanding and "**talking to**" our four-legged friends – like horse whisperers, for example.

I am the first to admit that I am no expert in animal communication, though if I ever see an elephant or a donkey give a speech to an audience, I might consider expanding my knowledge to include animal interactions.

Okay, so we have established the boundaries of this chapter – we are focusing only on skills needed for effective **HUMAN** communication.

We will build on the five vocal components you have learned about in this book, and then expand into other "**must-know**" elements of successful art of conveying your ideas to other people.

A good speaker CONTROLS all the vocal elements perfectly!

First, let's have another quick look at the all-important vocal components, this time- let's look at them from a speakers' percpective:

Pitch is how high or low your voice will sound in a given situation – an indication of your emotional state at that particular presentation or meeting.

Tone is an "attitude" *(both good and bad)* that you will try to convey using the sound of your voice. Think about the expression *"I didn't like his tone of voice."* So yes – it's not only **WHAT** you say, but also **HOW** you say it.

Volume is how quietly or loud you speak during your presentation – whispers, yells, and all the vocal ranges in between.

Pace is the speed (*or the slowness*) with which you decide to give your speech.

Rhythm is the evenness or unevenness of your voice, accent and your intonation. It is extremely important to keep your audience engaged and participating at all times without falling asleep!

I trust that you have committed these components to your memory and that you have practiced them after each chapter. **A good speaker** will incorporate all these elements every time he speaks because he knows how they can improve the presentation and ensure that the core message is being transmitted in the most efficient way possible.

Putting your thoughts into words

Before we get to the actual act of speaking, let's look at some other important elements of oral communication... You have an idea you want to convey: **you want other people to understand your message and recognize the value in what you are telling them**.

Many factors go into the making of a verbal message that will catch the listeners' attention and spark their interest. As we learned in a previous lesson - the 7%-38%-55% rule works here too. The first factor is the content and structure of the message (*the 7 percent of our message*). The second is delivery (*this is where the voice plays a major role and it stands for 38 percent*). And the third one consists of body language (*the 55 percent*).

Let's begin with the first part – the content, structure, and substance of your message.

I don't have to tell you that no matter how good your speaking skills are, they won't get you very far if the content of the message you are conveying has *no real value* to the listeners. By **"value"** I mean information that will, in some way, benefit other people - have a meaningful impact- or make a positive difference in their personal or professional lives.

So how do you **"package"** your ideas into a catchy and engaging message?

Here are some tips that should get you started:

Keep your message **clear and concise**, not cluttered with too many themes or unrelated details. A speech is meant to have <u>**one main point**</u>, and <u>**one (*your*) perspective**</u>, which will support your idea and inspire some action in others.

If you try to argue too many different points at once, your message will not be as effective or well received. Your audience may not think or analyze the way you do. They don't know everything you've been through and understand what lies behind each aspect of your speech. They can - however - grasp your idea if it's **simple and concentrated**.

Here's an example:

Say you are encouraging your listeners to adopt homeless pets from your community's animal shelter. This is how your presentation should be structured-

• **State the problem**: The shelter currently houses 50 abandoned dogs and cats. The animals are found in the streets, but the shelter checks them for medical problems and makes sure they are healthy, fed, and generally well taken care of.

• **Let the listeners know what will happen if action is not taken**: If the pets are *not* adapted, they will eventually be euthanized because the shelter's capacity is limited.

• **Call to action**: Tell the audience how a shelter pet can improve their lives- companionship, unconditional love, etc.

You will make a powerful impression if you share your *own story* of adoption, and let the listeners know how the pet you brought from the shelter into your home has made your life better. Try to cite a couple of anecdotes or specific examples to illustrate the point.

In conclusion

I have added up the 'DO' and 'DON'T DO' of what I've learned as a keynote speaker throughout the years. Memorize it and know it by heart:

DO-

• **Lay out the facts**, outlining the problem as you make your audience interested in the story and understand how it relates to *THEM*.

• **Mention a solution** to the problem and, where appropriate, how you propose to resolve it in an efficient way. This is also the part where you actually *"unite"* with them and make them understand that they, too, are an inseparable part of your subject.

• **Inspire the action**- because no speech is complete without a *"call to action."* In fact, if you finish a speech or any type of communication, **even with a friend**, without having some sort of a *"call to action"* by the end, you are missing the concept of communication and you stay in the *"**comfort zone**"* of shallow speeches and bad communication skills. **If that's the case, you could just as well say nothing!**

DON'T DO-

- **Stray away from facts** into assumptions, suppositions, and guesses.

- Talk about things that are **not related to the topic** or clutter the presentation with irrelevant details. That happens a lot when you're not focused, too relaxed or even worse - when you simply don't know the subject of discussion thoroughly enough!

- **Never, ever lie** about anything. If you're not sure or don't know something, say it. Be humble and truthful. Say, **"I'm not sure,"** or **"I don't know,"** and even go another step and ask, **"what do YOU think about it?"** or **"know about it?"**

Now go back and read this chapter again. And again. Until you understand the meaning behind every element of a good speech. If I will wake you up in the middle of the night- you should be able to repeat everything you've learned here by heart!

Once you've mastered the above mentioned rules, move on to the next chapter.

Strong introduction & conclusion

Every part of your message is important, but the **beginning and the end** should be especially compelling. That's because the introduction serves to grab the listeners' attention or "**hook**" them and let them know what points and arguments you will cover in your presentation. And the **conclusion** is the last chance to re-emphasize your core message.

This brief video explains these points really well:

 18 | www.5j.biz/voice/18

So for the best impact:

Begin with an attention-catching story, anecdote, or any other strong statement that provides a lead-in to your argument.

I stumbled upon this great guy who really shows how to start with the right mood! Check this video and pay attention to the Paypee Tovary aspects of his voice in the first version of his "*opener*" and the aspects of his voice in the second, much better "*opener.*"

You'll immediately see in action what we've learned:

19 | www.5j.biz/voice/19

Finish with a forceful conclusion that briefly sums up, but not repeats, the main points. You may think you are doing your audience a favor by restating the same information over and over again, but excessive repetition only leads to loss of interest.

One of the most poignant and powerful conclusions I've ever heard is from **Apple** co-founder **Steve Jobs**. It very eloquently ends the speech he gave at the **Harvard University** commencement ceremony in 2005, six years before his death:

"Here's to the crazy ones. The misfits. The rebels. The troublemakers. The round pegs in the square holes.

The ones who see things differently. They're not fond of rules. And they have no respect for the status quo. You can quote them, disagree with them, glorify or vilify them.

About the only thing you can't do is ignore them. Because they change things. They invent. They imagine. They heal. They explore. They create. They inspire. They push the human race forward.

Maybe they have to be crazy.

How else can you stare at an empty canvas and see a work of art? Or sit in silence and hear a song that's never been written? Or gaze at a red planet and see a laboratory on wheels?

We make tools for these kinds of people.

While some see them as the crazy ones, we see genius. Because the people who are crazy enough to think they can change the world, are the ones who do."

Mastering the above-mentioned techniques takes some practice. So start by creating a presentation putting forth a thought or an idea and shape it along the lines mentioned above. Once you sharpen this particular skill, you are ready to move to the second factor: **delivery**.

Be well-spoken

"Speak clearly, if you speak at all; carve every word before you let it fall."

~ *American author and poet Oliver Wendell Holmes*

Have you ever heard someone speak so passionately and articulately that his or her words really touched and inspired you? That's the kind of "**delivery**" you want to develop as well. There are many speeches that had made a strong and lasting impression on me, and I'd like to share one of them here. This is an excerpt of a presentation given to the General Assembly of the United Nations.

What is special about this particular speech is that it was delivered by a 16-year-old **Pakistani** teen, **Malala Yousafzai**, who was shot by the **Taliban** in October 2012 for being an outspoken advocate for girls' education. Her courage and activism have been an inspiration to millions around the world, and her communication skills are exemplary as well.

Just listen:

20 | www.5j.biz/voice/20

Aside from the thought-provoking content of her talk, note that her delivery – as far as the pitch, tone, volume, pace, and rhythm are concerned – is also **flawless**, which is an amazing feat for someone so young.

What makes Malala's speech so impressive besides the powerful message she is conveying, is that she is articulate and speaks clearly; she doesn't mumble or mutter.

Her voice projects well, her speech pattern has a flow and smoothness to it. And because of all these elements, she comes across as knowledgeable, confident, trustworthy, and in control of herself.

These are the exact same qualities that you or any effective communicator want to portray as well: **knowledge, confidence, trust, and control.**

How do you go about it?

Keep reading the next chapter in order to take a look at some of the techniques you need to master.

Making an impact!

Now that you know the importance of each of the five vocal components, use them to "sweeten" your speech and gain the power and strength of a "**leader**," to really leave a strong impression on your audience or followers:

Pay attention to the pitch.

Questions should go up in pitch at the end while affirmative statements should end on a lower note. When you're getting excited and sharing a strong paragraph with a strong concept in it, raise your pitch and speak on a higher note than usual. It keeps the audience **on the edge of their seats**, understanding that you're leading them into a sort of a "**climax**."

Learn to use the tone effectively.

Even the best messages can fail to deliver if you emphasize the *wrong* words. Remember what you learned in the chapter about the tone: the wrong one can make you enemies rather than friends.

What is the main subject of your speech?

Highlight the words that support this subject

throughout the speech in your printed version. Ask yourself how to use your tone to put a special emphasis on these highlighted words.

Adjust the volume.

Vary the volume to prevent your voice from either being constantly loud or monotonous; variations in volume alert your listeners to the nuances of your message. It is a good idea to raise the volume a bit as you build toward a particularly important point and before you go higher in pitch, which will be done when you're getting to the climax of the story.

You should also control the volume of your fvoice in two main parts of your speech:

- **GO LOWER:** When you want everyone's attention to something very important and very crucial. Slow down the pace and lower your volume so everyone will have to work harder in order to listen to what you have to say.

Let's try it together - from here on, I want you to read these lines out loud. Yes, these very lines you're reading right now. Go ahead, read it out loud:

Good. I can hear you reading me now. **And now... comes the most important thing ever...** (*lower your volume as you read this*) I have realized (*lower it even more, almost whispering*) that this book ... can really ... really ... change the way I speak!

How did it feel? Did you understand the power of lowering your volume and pace? Did you see how you're getting more engaging and portraying an important point that **EVERYBODY** will want to hear?

• **GO LOUD:** So when do we go loud? A good example is when we want to portray a different character. So if we want to talk about someone else who left a strong impression on us, or harmed us, or anything else - as long as it is talking as if we were someone else!

So you basically say something like: "**And then this man approached me**..." second thing you do is go loud and say what he said to you. *No need to say to the audience: "Here's what he said..."* because simply by being loud all of a sudden, your audience will immediately understand you're doing a *character shift* and you're saying what that OTHER person told YOU!

Another good timing for speaking loud is when you need to get everyone's attention to something important. But this must be preceded by a short pause.

Your speech is flowing as you say: "**And we all know that being here is extremely important to our community but...**" (*here comes a few-second pause that generates interest in your audience and leaves them wondering why you stopped! Then you raise your volume and add the affirmative statement*) "**IT IS NOT ENOUGH JUST TO BE HERE! WE MUST TAKE ACTION OUTSIDE AS WELL**" or whatever it is you're trying to say.

Pace yourself.

Slow down the pace to stress certain ideas, and **quicken** it to show excitement. *DO NOT* speak too quickly without any variations of the pace because you will be perceived as nervous; if you speak excruciatingly slow throughout, you will bore your listeners and they will not be receptive to your message.

Use the RIGHT rhythm.

Make your sentences **ear-friendly** with rhythm suitable to **your** specific language, which means stressing the words that are important to the meaning of the sentence.

Pause to emphasize important points or to give listeners time to absorb a particular concept. Also pause when you're about to transition to another idea or when playing around with Paypee Tovary's vocal elements.

Some people are afraid to pause because it makes them worried that they might *"lose the crowd."* **Don't be worried**. Pausing is a powerful tool for a speaker. You may use a trick of having a glass or a bottle of water next to you. You then take advantage of it as you're pausing in order to sip from your drink... Once you'll get more confident you won't need this trick anymore, but it is always useful.

Infuse your voice with emotion appropriate for the message's content.

This will ensure your voice doesn't sound "**flat**" or *robotic*, but ebbs and recedes with meaning. If you wanted to pinpoint the reason why some speakers "**have it**" and others don't, that's where it hides!

The world's greatest speakers have emotion encrusted into each and every word that comes out of their mouths!

Rely on your diaphragm.

Use your stomach muscles to support your breath as you speak so that your voice is clear and steady. Place a hand over your stomach, just below your ribs -you should feel the muscles there move as you speak.

Look at the video of Malala one more time and see how she incorporates all these components into her speech. This proves that young people can teach us a great deal about effective communication!

Okay, so now you know what you need to pay attention to while you speak. Let's have a look at the things you **SHOULDN'T** do...

Blunders to avoid

There are things you should never ever do when giving a speech or trying to use the methods I taught you in this book to influence others. Never commit these common mistakes because they will spoil even the best speech:

DON'T sound as if you're ending each sentence with a question (the so-called *"upward inflection"*). For instance, instead of saying *"I have extensive experience in management,"* you say *"I have extensive experience in management???"* Notice that this sentence is not intended to be a question, but your style of speaking might make it sound this way.

Why is this bad? When you are telling people something of importance, you want to sound credible and, as mentioned above, knowledgeable, confident, trustworthy, and in control. But the *upward inflection* makes you sound just the opposite - unsure of yourself and incapable of communicating your ideas convincingly.

DON'T overuse filler words such as *"like," "you know,"* or **"um, uh, er, ah.**" For example, if you pepper your presentation with sentences such as: **"I am, like, real happy that you came to hear me speak, and, you know, I will teach you some cool**

stuff, like, er, how to speak, um, effectively."

Need I even tell you why this is a "**no-no**?" Think about it: by sounding juvenile and inarticulate, do you actually expect anyone to take you seriously and be responsive to your message?

There are some more pitfalls to be avoided, and I will cover them in the next section, which pertains to…

…**the body language!**

Body Language Tips

Body language conveys messages through posture, gestures, mannerisms, and facial expressions. All kinds of emotions and mindsets – anger, hostility, insecurity, anxiety, as well as confidence – can be gleaned from the body language. When you are speaking to a group, you want to appear calm, confident, and in control. To accomplish that, you need to adapt certain postures, gestures, and expressions that will, together with your vocal skills, wow your audience:

Stand straight.

Not only will your voice project better, but you will also be seen as someone who is in command. Slouching, on the other hand, will indicate that you are unsure of yourself – not the best way to inspire people! Have you ever seen a speaker moving from one side of the stage to the other time after time? This is extremely annoying and makes your eyes tired. No to mention that your neck might get broken! Don't 'dance' around the stage unless you are trying to convey a certain message by doing this.

Look directly at your audience.

Eye contact is absolutely essential when you are communicating your ideas. It creates a sense of directness and sincerity, whereas avoiding eye contact means you are distancing yourself from your audience. How do you expect to "**sell**" your ideas to these people, when you are avoiding any interaction with them?

Adapt suitable facial expressions.

If your speech is light-hearted, smile often. Smile is the best way to win people over to your cause. A friendly demeanor makes you more approachable and people will pay more attention to someone who looks and sounds friendly.

Involve the hands.

You can use hand gestures to enhance your presentation and reinforce the key points. Notice how Malala uses her hands at the end of her speech when she talks about "**one child, one teacher, one book**."

What are the things you shouldn't do?

Even though I mentioned that you should have a straight posture and not slouch, and not to run from one side of the stage to another- this doesn't mean you should be rigid and stand like a statue. **No, no, no!** You should have fluid and graceful - rather than clumsy - motions of the entire body, which will liven up your presentation. If you're excited: **GET EXCITED**. Just don't overact it!

In other words – be natural, be relaxed, and be engaged! If you're 100% present, your audience will feel it and will be there with you - in body and in spirit!

So now that you know the basics of successful communication, take the time to practice each step. Use the knowledge you learned in this chapter, as well as in all the previous ones, to whip your verbal communication skills into the best shape possible.

I hope you've learned all the different aspects of the voice and practiced on analyzing them!

I want to thank you for being such an interested and attentive student, please, take a minute and leave a review for this book on Amazon.com! It means a lot to me.

Feel free to share your thoughts and comments about my book by emailing me using the contact page on my website: www.mentalizer.com.

Made in the USA
Monee, IL
16 November 2020